Unit C

Stage and Screen

Using Light and Sound

I WONDER

Colored lights flash. The deep sounds of the bass mix with the richness of the piano. What can you ask to find out how light, sound, and electricity are used to televise a concert? What can you ask to find out how these things are used for producing a news broadcast?

Work with a partner to make a list of your questions. Be ready to share your list with the rest of the class.

Recording studio's sound-mixing console

TV news crew

C3

I PLAN

You may have asked questions such as those below as you wondered about the making of a televised event. Scientists also ask questions about light, sound, and electricity. Then they plan ways to find answers to their questions. Now you and your classmates can plan how you will investigate the ways light, sound, and electricity interact during stage and screen events.

My Science Log

How do the stage lights change colors?

How does a video camera work?

How does the picture get from the camera to a TV set?

How is sound transmitted?

With Your Class

Plan how your class will use the activities and readings from the **I Investigate** part of this unit. What other resources can you use?

On Your Own

There are many ways to learn about light, sound, and electricity. Following are some things you can do to explore light, sound, and electricity by yourself or with some classmates. Some explorations may take longer to do than others. Look over the suggestions and choose . . .

- **Places to Visit**
- **Projects to Do**
- **Books to Read**

PLACES TO VISIT

EXPLORE A TV STUDIO

Visit a local TV studio to see how a news program is produced with the latest equipment. Contact the studio's public relations department to arrange for a tour. Before you go, make a list of questions to ask. Find out all you can about the people who work together to put on a broadcast.

DISCOVER THE SCIENCE OF SOUND

Plan a visit to a local musical instrument store. Arrange for someone at the store to demonstrate both acoustic and electronic instruments. Find out how each instrument produces sound. Compare an electric guitar and a nonelectric guitar.

ATTEND A LIVE PERFORMANCE

Many communities have amateur or professional theaters. Check the schedule of a theater near you. Arrange to attend a play with friends or relatives. As you enjoy the performance, pay attention to how light and sound are used to help set the mood in the play.

PROJECTS TO DO

KEEPING AN EYE ON LIGHT

Make a drawing of one outdoor place at different times of day—even by moonlight, if you can. Notice how the shadows and the colors change. Explain why filmmakers need to use artificial light to change the way things appear. Describe how filmmakers might use artificial light.

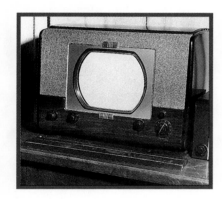

DISCOVERING OUR HISTORY

How many TV sets were in American homes in 1930? in 1940? How many are there today? Find out and make a graph to show the increase in numbers of TVs from 1930 through 1990. Then find out how TV has changed people's lives. Talk to an older relative or neighbor who remembers the time before TV. Share your discoveries with your class.

CHOOSE AN INVENTOR

Who was Lewis Howard Latimer? What did Philo Farnsworth and Vladimir K. Zworykin do? Science is about wondering and discovering. Find out about some of the people who have helped us learn more about light, sound, and electricity. Make a poster to share what you've learned.

BOOKS TO READ

Backstage with Clawdio

by Harriet Berg Schwartz (Knopf, 1993).

This book introduces you to Clawdio the cat. It's a good thing he is backstage to make sure things for the play run smoothly. The play needs lighting, moving scenery, and even a flying Peter Pan. Putting it together takes a lot of work; special equipment; knowledge; and, of course, one cat to see that everyone does the job right.

Look Alive: Behind the Scenes of an Animated Film

by Elaine Scott (William Morrow, 1992). Have you ever read Beverly Cleary's books about Ralph S. Mouse? Someone made a movie of one, *Ralph S. Mouse.* Could you train a mouse to act and to ride a motorcycle? Of course not. So the movie was photographed with actors for the human roles and a movable model for Ralph. The movie is great! This book tells how it was done.

More Books to Read

Mirrors: Finding Out About the Properties of Light

by Bernie Zubrowski (William Morrow, 1992), Outstanding Science Trade Book. Anyone who understands how light travels and who uses mirrors to reflect and bend the light can create many special effects and tricks. These effects can be used when putting on shows, playing tricks, or learning about light. This book shows you how this is done.

Exploring Electricity

by Ed Catherall (Steck-Vaughn, 1989). In this book, you will learn how electricity is made and how it is used. You will learn how to do simple experiments and some that are more difficult. You will find out how to make an electric motor, a battery with a lemon, and other projects. Electricity is important in our lives. We depend upon it in many ways.

Sound Waves to Music

by Neil Ardley (Gloucester Press, 1990). Sound is all around you. There are even sounds that you cannot hear. Sound can be so strong that it will make things move. Sound can be copied and stored. Sound can affect the way you feel. We can take pictures with sound. Read this book to find out why there is a lot more to sound than just hearing it.

The Chinese Mirror

by Mirra Ginsburg (Harcourt Brace, 1988). Suppose you were looking into a mirror for the first time. What would you think when you saw your reflection? This story, a tale from Korea, tells of the misunderstandings that occur when a man brings a mirror from China into his village. The people have never looked in a mirror before, and each person resents the stranger viewed in the glass. Read to find out what happens when the mirror is shattered.

INVESTIGATE

To find answers to their questions, scientists read, think, talk to others, and do experiments. Their investigations often lead to new questions.

In this unit, you will have many chances to think and work like a scientist. How will you find answers to questions you posed?

▶ **HYPOTHESIZING** You form a hypothesis when you want to explain how or why something happens. Your hypothesis is an explanation based on what you already know. A hypothesis should be tested in an experiment.

▶ **COMPARING** When you compare objects or events, you look for what they have in common. You also look for differences between them.

▶ **EXPERIMENTING** You experiment to test hypotheses. In a test, you must control variables and gather accurate data. You also must interpret the data and draw conclusions.

Are you ready to begin?

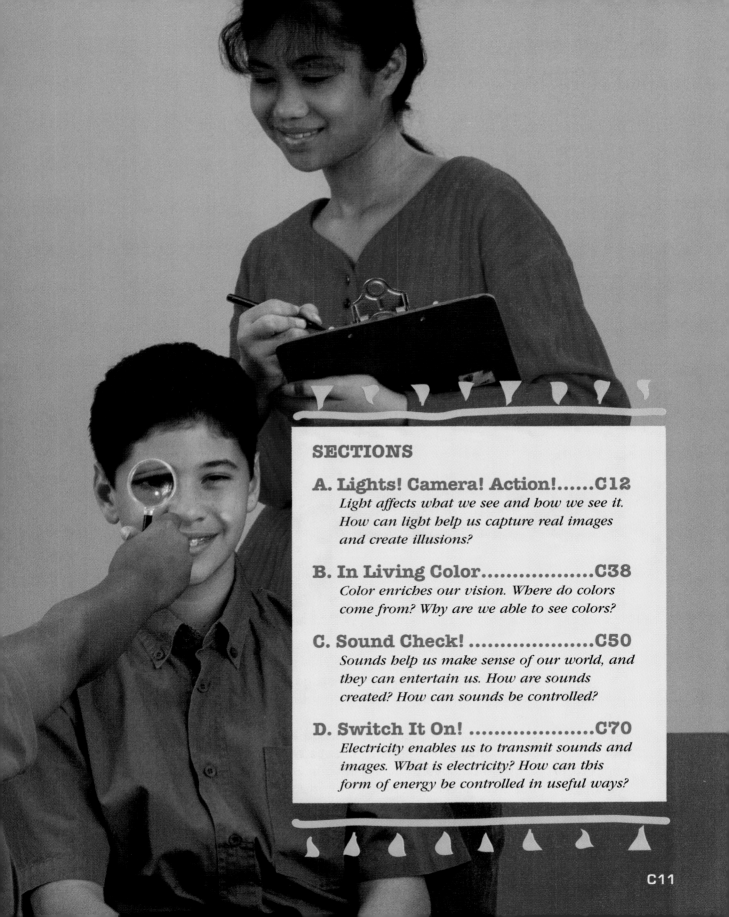

SECTIONS

SECTION A
Lights! Camera! Action!

▲ TV camera operator

Think about something exciting you have seen on TV. While you were watching, did you think about science? Maybe not, but science plays an important role in bringing the program to you. This section will take you behind the scenes of events on stage and screen. You'll explore the characteristics of light that enable us to see and to produce exciting visual effects.

What equipment helps people create stage and screen events? How does this equipment use light to create what we see? As you begin to explore and discover, record in your Science Log how you think light is used to create visual special effects you have seen.

1 BEHIND THE SCENES

The image on your TV set is the end of the long process of bringing a show from the stage to you. Light and images are carefully controlled to give the visual effects desired by the writers and producers. As you read, think about which part of the process you'd like to try.

PREPRODUCTION

PRODUCTION

▶ Every show begins with an idea. Producers and directors work together to plan how to present their ideas to an audience. Scriptwriters put the ideas on paper. These people are planning to produce a concert for TV.

▲ On the day of production, after many hours of setting up and rehearsing, the performers begin the show.

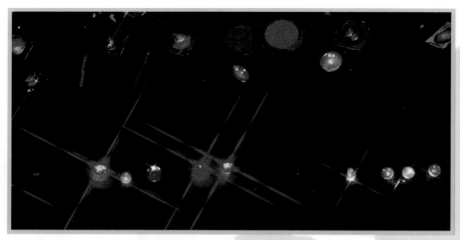

▲ Lights are used to light the stage and the performers, to create a mood, and to produce exciting special effects.

▶ The sound engineer listens as the sound is recorded from microphones placed on stage. The engineer uses the sound board to control the quality and level of the sound being recorded.

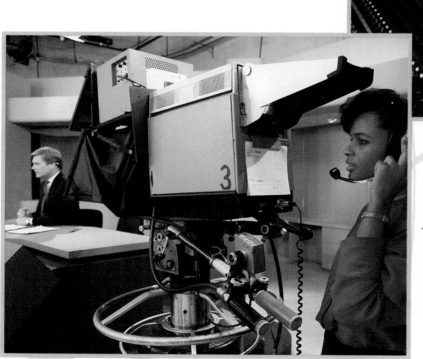

◀ At least one camera operator, or videographer, records the events on stage. The videographer controls the content and quality of the recorded image by adjusting the camera and its lens.

▲ The director watches the monitor to see what is being recorded on tape and gives each videographer directions. In a live show, the director works with an engineer to control which camera's picture is transmitted at each moment.

POST PRODUCTION

◀ The editors select and combine the best scenes to create the final program. The editors must pay attention to both the image and the sound. They may also put in special audio effects, such as a crowd cheering, or video effects, such as making an image spin onto the screen, for excitement.

▶ When the show is ready for transmission, it travels through cables as a series of electrical impulses. The cables carry the program to a transmitter, which sends signals to homes by way of antennas or another series of cables, or to a satellite for transmission around the world.

▼ Finally, the show reaches the TV in your home, where you can sit back and enjoy yourself. Today you're just a spectator, but in the near future, you will be able to use an interactive TV to interact with the characters in a program. TVs will become more like computers.

LESSON 1 REVIEW

Make a list of all of the ways that light, sound, and electricity are used to bring a show from a stage to your TV.

2 LIGHT AND SHADOWS

The scene opens with the street in darkness. Suddenly, as the sun breaks out from behind the clouds, light and shadows mix. In this lesson, you will discover how light travels.

Beyond the Shadows

Creating images with light and shadows can turn science into entertainment. As you read, try to picture how light and shadows help create the show.

SHADOW PUPPETS OF INDONESIA

by **Marjorie Jackson** from *Cricket*

After sundown in the island country of Indonesia, crowds gather in front of white screens to watch *wayang kulit* performances, the dramatic shadow puppet plays that have been a part of Indonesian culture for many hundreds of years. Cymbals clang and drums thump as fanged giants lumber across the screen. Everyone laughs to see clowns argue and bite each other's noses, or watch monkeys soar in wild games of leapfrog.

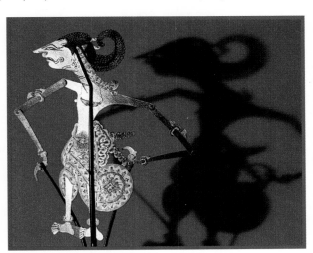

▲ **Indonesian puppet**

Wayang kulit is one of the most popular and entertaining arts of Indonesia. The plays are often staged in open courtyards, and once the music begins, the whole village stops to watch. Children perch in trees, and others sit on mats, but important guests are given chairs. Even today a *wayang* (the Indonesian word for shadow) performance is thought to work a special magic. A powerful *dalang*, or puppet master, is said to bring protection and good fortune to all who attend.

Each *wayang kulit* is a flat figure, cut out, hammered, and chiseled from dried water buffalo hide.

Today, a full set of *wayang kulit* might contain six hundred puppets, but usually only forty or fifty are needed at one performance. The *dalang* arrives wearing a printed sarong and headcloth. He sits cross-legged next to the screen, on the side away from the audience, and takes his puppets from their box. He then spreads incense over them. A bright coconut oil lamp hangs overhead to cast the puppets' shadows onto the screen. The light shimmers and makes the puppets' shadows come to life and move. Today an electric light bulb is often used instead. Since its

light is steady, the *dalang* gently shakes the puppets to make them move. The puppet master moves new characters quickly on or off stage so that his hands won't cast shadows. A figure appears to become smaller when he moves it toward the screen, and then it blurs when he pulls it away. At the moment of blurring, the *dalang* can exchange two puppets, giving the illusion of changing a beautiful maiden into an ogre, or a lion into a knight.

At sunrise the final gong is sounded. Some of the crowd are caught napping. The puppets fade from the screen and are folded into their box. Everyone has laughed and cried, and now they will go home content. The *wayang kulit* performance was a success. It has been "written in the world," as the Indonesians say, and its goodness will be lasting.

THINK ABOUT IT

How are the shadow puppet show and the TV concert alike? How are they different?

A C T I V I T Y

Shadow Play

The *dalang* entertains his audience with shadow puppets. Now, you can entertain your classmates with a shadow puppet show.

DO THIS

1. Make a puppet by cutting a shape out of cardboard. Use tape to attach the puppet to a thin stick.

2. Hang the sheet from the ceiling or over a doorway.

3. Place the light about 2 m away from the back of the sheet.

4. **CAUTION: Do not touch the hot light.** Turn on the light. Direct the beam toward the sheet.

5. Darken the room by closing the shades and turning off most of the lights.

6. Do the following with a partner and record your observations.

   - Hold the puppet behind the light. Is there a shadow?

   - Hold the puppet between the light and the sheet. What happens?

   - Take the puppet from between the light source and the sheet. Move the light source away from the sheet. What happens to the brightness and the area of the light?

   - Move the light source closer to the sheet. What happens to the brightness and the area of the light?

THINK AND WRITE

How do light and a puppet create a shadow? Draw a labeled diagram to show your ideas.

MATERIALS
- cardboard
- scissors
- tape
- sticks
- white sheet
- gooseneck lamp
- Science Log data sheet

How Does Light Travel?

Think about how the light and the puppet worked together to create the images in your shadow puppet theater. You can use a model to show this and to explain how shadows are cast.

Light travels in a straight line. Your puppet blocked the rays of light and cast a shadow on the sheet. A shadow forms when something blocks a source of light like a flashlight, a projector, or the sun. A *ray model* like the one below can help you see how the light traveled in your shadow theater.

In the diagram, notice how the rays spread out as they get farther away from the light source. When the rays are spread out, the light is less bright than when the rays are close together. You probably discovered that the light became brighter as you moved the light source closer to the sheet in your theater. How would the puppet's shadow look in bright light?

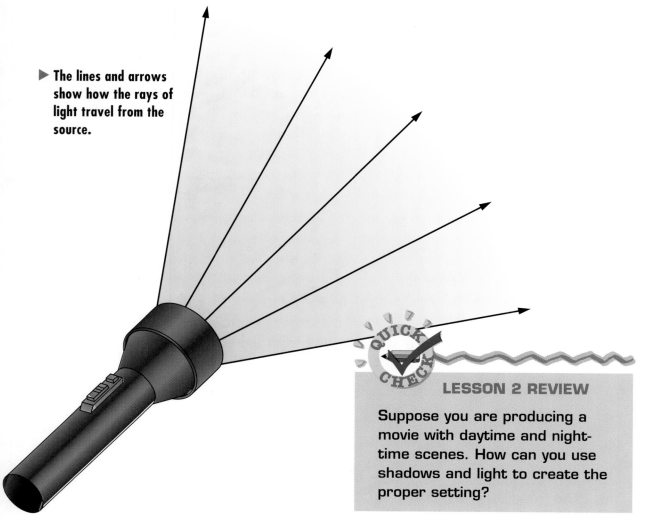

► The lines and arrows show how the rays of light travel from the source.

QUICK CHECK

LESSON 2 REVIEW

Suppose you are producing a movie with daytime and night-time scenes. How can you use shadows and light to create the proper setting?

3 HOW LIGHT IS REFLECTED

When you look in a mirror, you see yourself. This experience shows one way in which light behaves. In this lesson, you will discover how light is reflected.

Stage Lights

Stage and screen producers use behaviors of light to produce interesting visual effects. The following passage describes some of the ways people work with stage lighting.

from *Ramona: Behind the Scenes of a TV Show* by Elaine Scott

 The lights that illuminate the set can be adjusted in hundreds of different ways. During blocking, Doug decides how much light he wants and where he wants it, and then he asks the lighting gaffer, Gary Phipps, to trim the lights accordingly. The gaffer is the person who is in charge of the lights, and the lighting grip is the person who helps the gaffer by moving the lights from place to place.

When a camera operator talks to a gaffer, it is almost as if they were conversing in an alien language.

"Barn-door that inkie off the wall, will you, Phipps?" asks Doug, and Phipps turns to his grip and asks him to climb up on a kitchen cabinet to adjust a black reflector (that does

▲ A grip adjusting lights

indeed look a bit like a barn door) over the "inkie," a 750-watt light, until the light shines exactly where Doug wants it.

By carefully moving the reflectors, the gaffer can create shadows on walls and take shadows away from faces. Different-colored filters, called gels, can be placed over the lights to give the scene a different mood. Filters placed over the lens of the camera can also change the lighting. For example, a special filter on the camera can change the ordinary flame of a candle into a star-shaped glow.

THINK ABOUT IT

Briefly describe what a gaffer needs to know about using light.

ACTIVITY

Just Passing Through

You've just read how the gaffer on a TV production crew changes the look of a set by adjusting light in different ways. Try this activity to see how different materials allow different amounts of light to pass through.

DO THIS

1 Darken the room, and shine the flashlight down onto a tabletop. Observe how much light falls on the tabletop.

2 Place each material one at a time over the lens of the flashlight, and shine the beam in the same place as before. Observe how much light falls on the tabletop.

THINK AND WRITE

COMPARING Comparing involves telling how objects are alike and how they are different. Which of the materials from this activity are most alike? Which are most different?

Traveling Light Rays Different materials allow different amounts of light to pass through. If all of the light from a light source passes through, the material is *transparent*. If some light passes through, the material is *translucent*. If no light passes through, the material is *opaque*. Use these definitions to classify the materials you tested in the activity.

MATERIALS
- flashlight
- clear plastic
- tissue paper
- colored cellophane
- black poster board
- Science Log data sheet

Bouncing Light Rays

When light hits the smooth, flat surface of a mirror, it bounces, or reflects. See if you can predict the direction in which light rays will reflect.

DO THIS

1 Attach the mirror to the wall at chest level or lower. Stand 1 to 2 m away from the mirror, off to one side. From this spot, you will be shining the beam of your flashlight toward the mirror. Before you turn the flashlight on, ask a partner to stand where you think the rays of light will be reflected by the mirror.

2 Darken the room, and shine the flashlight so that its beam hits the mirror. Do the light rays bounce to where your partner is standing? If not, have your partner move to where the light rays do reflect. Experiment with different locations for you and your partner.

3 For each trial, draw a ray diagram to show the path of light from the flashlight to the mirror to your partner.

THINK AND WRITE

EXPERIMENTING When you experiment, you gather and interpret data and draw conclusions. Examine your ray diagrams. Describe how the angle at which light rays strike the mirror compares with the angle at which the rays reflect off it.

Multiply with Mirrors

You've discovered how mirrors reflect light. Now, in this activity, you will use mirrors to produce special effects.

DO THIS

MATERIALS
- **2 small, flat mirrors**
- **tape**
- **eraser or other small object**
- **Science Log data sheet**

1 Tape the mirrors together side by side so that they can be folded to face each other.

2 Unfold the mirrors and stand them upright. Place the object so that it faces the unfolded mirrors in front of where they are joined. Count the reflections of the object.

3 Fold the mirrors slightly to form a very wide V shape. Count the reflections of the object.

4 Gently move the mirrors to make the V narrower. Observe how the number of reflections changes.

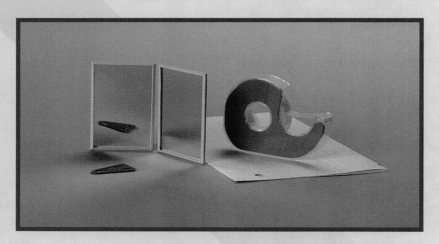

THINK AND WRITE

How would you explain the changes in the number of reflections as you folded the mirrors?

Take a Look at Yourself

Try this activity to see how differently shaped mirrors reflect light and form images.

DO THIS

Look at your reflection in each mirror, try the following, and record your observations.

MATERIALS
- flat mirror
- convex mirror
- concave mirror
- Science Log data sheet

- Describe the image in the mirror. Is the image smaller than, the same size as, or larger than your face? Is the image right side up or upside down?

- Describe where the image in the mirror appears to be: on the surface of the mirror or behind it.

- Move the mirror left, right, backward, and forward. What happens to the image?

- Touch your right cheek. Which cheek does the image in the mirror touch?

THINK AND WRITE

1. Compare the images formed by the three mirrors.

2. How might a convex mirror be used on a school bus? Explain how the image formed by the mirror fits the use.

Reflecting on Reflection

Here are the answers to some of the questions you might have about the activities you've done in this lesson.

Q: How can a gaffer tell where a ray of light will be reflected?

A: Think of light as traveling like a basketball. Basketball players know that once the ball hits the backboard, it must move at a certain angle to go into the hoop. A gaffer knows that when light hits something, like a mirror, it bounces in much the same way a ball would. The ray of light hits the mirror and bounces off at equal angles.

Q: Why can I see myself in a mirror?

A: When you look in a flat mirror, light rays bounce off your body to the mirror and back. Since the surface of the mirror is smooth, most of the rays are reflected back to your eyes in the same direction.

    Curved mirrors reflect images differently than flat mirrors do. That's why your images in the concave and convex mirrors look different from your image in a flat mirror. Concave mirrors are curved inward. Convex mirrors are curved outward.

Q: Why don't all objects reflect light as a mirror does?

A: Most objects are not smooth like a mirror. When light rays strike a rough surface, they are reflected back in different directions. That's why on a windy day, you can't see your reflection in a lake. The rough surface of the water scatters the light in many directions. On a calm day, though, a lake can act like a mirror, reflecting the rays of light back to you in a single direction.

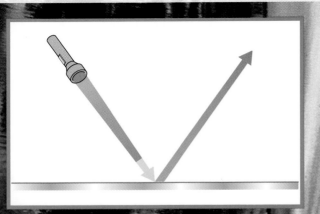

QUICK CHECK

LESSON 3 REVIEW

Describe one "special effect" you could create using filters and each of these mirrors: flat, concave, and convex.

4 LIGHT AND LENSES

You've explored ways that light rays reflect in straight lines. Can light rays bend? Light rays and camera lenses produce some surprising sights.

ACTIVITY

How Lenses Bend Light

What kind of lens is used in a camera? This activity can help you find out.

DO THIS

1 Place the light source more than a meter away from where you are working. Turn on the light source. Hold the convex lens above the zero end of the meter stick so that light from the source passes through the lens.

2 Move the sheet of paper along the meter stick until the light rays form a pinpoint of light. This is the focal point.

3 Measure the distance between the center of the lens and the pinpoint of light. This is the focal length.

4 Hold the convex lens close to this page, at a distance less than the focal length. What do you observe? Where does the image appear in relation to the paper?

5 Hold the concave lens in the path of your light source, as in step 1. What happens to the rays of light?

THINK AND WRITE

Compare what convex and concave lenses do to light.

C27

Can You Believe Your Eyes?

A movie character sees a mirage in a desert scene. What causes a mirage? Read and examine the pictures to find out.

Think about how it feels to walk through deep water. Your legs have to work much harder than usual, and you can't move as fast as on dry ground. When light rays travel from one medium to another, they change speed, too. This change sometimes causes the rays to bend, or *refract*.

Have you ever seen a mirage on a hot day? This is an example of refraction, too. Light refracts when it travels through air of different temperatures. If the air just above the ground is hotter than the surrounding air, the sunlight is refracted, creating an optical illusion on the surface. Refracted light may create images that surprise you, but refraction follows very predictable rules.

▲ One straw or two?

◀ Mirage

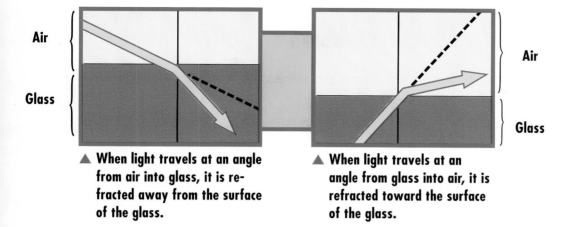

Air

Glass

▲ When light travels at an angle from air into glass, it is refracted away from the surface of the glass.

Air

Glass

▲ When light travels at an angle from glass into air, it is refracted toward the surface of the glass.

Understanding how light refracts has helped people create lenses to refract light in useful ways. Look at the instruments pictured here, and tell what each does.

▼ Binoculars   ▼ Eyeglasses   ▼ Camera

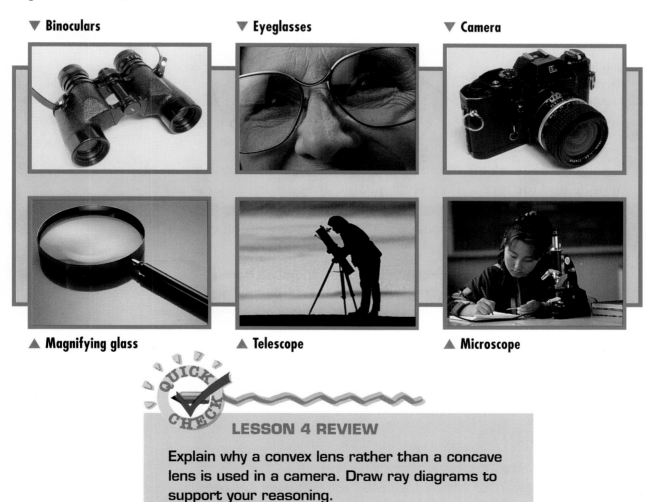

▲ Magnifying glass   ▲ Telescope   ▲ Microscope

QUICK CHECK

LESSON 4 REVIEW

Explain why a convex lens rather than a concave lens is used in a camera. Draw ray diagrams to support your reasoning.

5 HOW WE SEE

No performance is complete without a viewing audience.
In this lesson, you will find out how people see.

Taking a Look at the Eye

You turn on the TV and watch your favorite program. Here is how you see it.

The lens refracts light rays to come together and form an upside-down image on the retina.

Light passes through the pupil and enters the lens. Muscles change the focal length of the lens by adjusting its thickness.

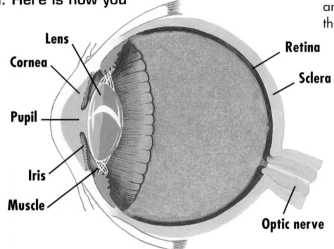

Lens
Cornea
Pupil
Iris
Muscle
Retina
Sclera
Optic nerve

The nerve cells of the retina send impulses to the brain. The brain interprets the image and you see it right side up.

Sometimes the shape of the eye causes images to form in front of or behind the retina. Then some people must use eyeglasses or contact lenses. Lenses correct vision problems by adjusting the refraction so that the rays come together at a focal point on each retina.

▼ Eyeballs that are too long form images in front of the retinas. The person is nearsighted and can't see faraway objects clearly.

▼ Eyeballs that are too short form images behind the retinas. The person is farsighted and can't see nearby objects clearly.

THINK ABOUT IT

What kind of lens, concave or convex, is used to correct for nearsightedness? for farsightedness? Explain your answers.

ACTIVITY

Eyeball to Eyeball

You look through your eyes at the world around you, but when was the last time you looked at your eyes?

MATERIALS
- flat mirror
- colored pencils
- hand lens
- penlight
- Science Log data sheet

DO THIS 🔆

1 Look at your eye in a mirror. Use colored pencils to draw what you see. Label the pupil, sclera (white area), iris, and cornea.

2 Look at another student's eye from the side. Can you see the clear bulge of the cornea in the eye?

3 Use a hand lens to look at the other student's eye under magnification. Compare what you see with what you noticed in your own eye.

4 Look at the pupil of the other student's eye, first in a brightly lit part of the room and then in a dark part of the room. What do you observe?

5 **CAUTION: Be careful not to press against or jab at your closed eyelid.** Darken the room. Turn the penlight on, and place it against the outer corner of your closed upper eyelid. Gently but firmly wiggle the penlight back and forth. Do you see the blood vessels on the back of your retina? Add these to your drawing.

THINK AND WRITE

Why are you unable to see well for a few minutes when you walk from a well-lighted room into a dark room? Why does your vision gradually improve?

Create Your Own Picture Show

Did you know that a movie is really just a series of still images, or frames? You can make an animated feature of your own with just a little drawing ability and with a trick played on your vision by your eyes.

MATERIALS
- at least 20 index cards
- colored pencils
- stapler
- white sheet of paper
- Science Log data sheet

DO THIS

1. Decide what you want to show in your animated feature. Here are some suggestions: the sun rising, a ball bouncing, a bird flying.

2. On each card, draw a tiny step in the action you want to show.

3. Put the cards in order from last to first. Staple the cards together at the side to form a book.

4. Flip the pages of the book, starting with the last page, and watch your drawings in action. Share your animated book with your classmates.

THINK AND WRITE

What appeared to happen to your drawings as you flipped the pages of your book? Why do you think this happened?

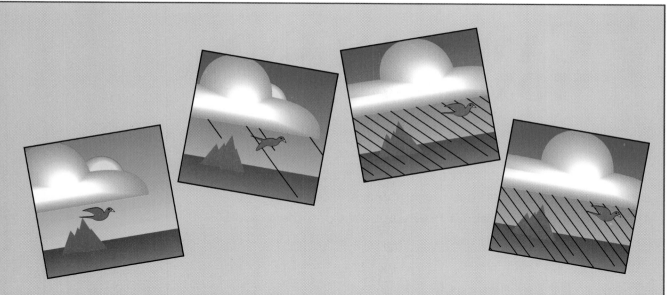

Visual Images   The figures in motion pictures appear to be moving because of *persistence of vision*. The retina of your eye can retain an image for a brief amount of time. If the images move quickly enough, one image blends into the next and you don't notice the empty space separating the images. Stare at the picture of stars and circles for at least 30 seconds. Then, immediately look at a white sheet of paper. What do you see on the paper? Why do you see this?

LESSON 5 REVIEW

In a movie, a nearsighted character starts a fire with her eyeglasses. At the same time, she describes in detail the small insect crawling up her arm. Is this possible? Explain your reasoning.

6 CAMERAS AND MOVIES

So far in this section, you've explored some of the science involved in creating and seeing both still and moving images. Now take a closer look at the technology that helps bring it all together. As you find out more about still cameras and motion pictures, think about how you might use these tools to create images of your own.

The Birth of Photography

This article describes the beginnings of photography in America. As you read, try to imagine what it must have been like for people to see their own images captured permanently for the first time.

THE DAGUERREOTYPE IN AMERICA

by June L. Sargent from *Cobblestone*

 Joseph Nicéphore Niépce took the earliest existing photograph in 1826 in France. Other experimenters, like Thomas Wedgewood, had produced images, but Niépce was the first to make them permanent.

Louis Jacques Mandé Daguerre was a stage designer in Paris who coproduced the diorama, a highly successful picture show that used special light effects. In an effort to find a mechanical method of producing pictures, Daguerre became Niépce's partner in 1829. But before Niépce's heliographic (etched by sunlight) process could be perfected, Niépce died.

By 1837, Daguerre produced a permanent photographic image. The daguerreotype, a silver-coated copper plate (sensitized by fuming with vapors of iodine), recorded a sharp image within a half hour when exposed to sunlight. Although the daguerreotype was expensive and laborious to prepare, it produced amazingly fine details and became extremely popular, especially in America.

Making a daguerreotype took a long time. A person could be required to sit still for approximately three minutes (some sittings could be longer). Any slight movement could distort the daguerreotype's image. To ensure that a subject did not move, a chair was developed that held the neck securely with a vise (a clamping device). Sometimes wrists and ankles were also strapped to the chair. In full-length daguerreotypes, a metal base can be seen behind the subject's feet.

The daguerreotype was important in the cultural development of America. It also helped the country make the transition from an agricultural to a technological society. Families afraid of separation by death could now obtain permanent images of

▲ Louis Daguerre

themselves together. Portraits of such famous personalities as Andrew Jackson, Edgar A. Poe, Jenny Lind, and Tom Thumb made

▲ Daguerreotype from the 1850s

them more real to the public. With the aid of the camera, the average American family could now view such exotic and faraway places as Africa, China, and Japan for the first time. The daguerreotype also became the eye of history, recording many important events.

Frontier photographers, like Robert H. Vance, were pioneers in a double sense. They explored a wild and

unsettled country and practiced a new science. Their daguerreotypes (prints made from negatives on glass were also used) of frontier towns, riverboats, miners, and Native Americans captured and preserved the adventurous flavor of life in the American West. As a result, hundreds of thousands of people migrated westward in search of golden opportunities.

The work of daguerreotypists helped educate the American people about themselves, their society, and the world. These early photographers can be considered artists, scientists, and historians all at the same time.

THINK ABOUT IT

How have photographs and movies helped you understand something about your family or the world around you? Tell how you think this technology makes a difference in our lives today.

How a Camera Works

Still cameras and film have changed dramatically since the time of the daguerreotype. As you look at the diagram below, think about ways in which the camera is similar to the human eye.

The *shutter speed control* lets you decide how long the shutter should be open to let light into the camera. Slower shutter speeds let in more light. You'd need a slower shutter speed on a cloudy day. Faster shutter speeds work better on a sunny day.

The *viewfinder* lets you look at an image before photographing it.

The *pentaprism* has mirrors to reflect the image you are photographing so that you can see it right side up. (The image is inverted when the light rays are refracted through the lens.)

The *release button* opens the shutter to let light into the camera.

The *aperture control* lets you adjust the amount of light coming into the camera. On a cloudy day, you might set the aperture to use the full diameter of the lens and let in plenty of light. On a bright day, you'd set the aperture to use less of the lens.

The *film* is a piece of plastic treated with light-sensitive chemicals. The light rays form a pattern on the film that is later developed to show the image.

The *lens,* or more often a series of lenses, refracts the rays of light to converge in a focal point on the film.

THINK ABOUT IT

Suppose you photograph a dimly lit indoor scene and later photograph a speeding race car in bright sunlight. How might your aperture control settings and your shutter speed control settings change?

Rana Segal:
Cinematographer

What is it like to be behind the eye of a camera? As you read the following, think about how the job described balances creativity with an understanding of technology.

Rana Segal became a filmmaker ten years ago. Now specializing in cinematography, Segal expresses her ideas on film. "I like creating beautiful images," explains Segal, "and cinematography is creating visual art."

▲ **Rana Segal shooting a scene**

Long before the camera starts to roll, Segal is involved in planning the shoot. "We sit down and decide how we want to convey the story with images. We deal with whether a shot will be a moving shot; a zoom or a close-up; a medium shot or a wide shot," explains Segal. She and her co-workers also discuss lighting.

"When we go to production, we are applying what we've already decided," says Segal. The production crew carries out the plan. Segal enjoys "working with a group to bring the project together."

Segal also works with many people outside of the film industry. "My favorite projects involve working with people

who explore other cultures through film," says Segal. "One of the things I like about filmmaking is that it seems like a good way to continue the learning process."

Segal has some advice for aspiring cinematographers. "When you go to the movies, pay attention. Look at the lighting and what the camera is doing. But most of all," says Segal, "you have to have persistence. If you really want to do it, keep working at it."

LESSON 6 REVIEW

Compare and contrast the human eye with a camera.

 DOUBLE CHECK

SECTION A REVIEW

Suppose you film your own movie. Describe how you would use light and shadow, mirrors, lenses, and cameras.

SECTION B
In Living Color

How do colors affect what you see?
Why do you think some photographers choose to take photographs in color, some like to take them in black and white, and some prefer to use colored filters?

In this section, you'll explore how colors are formed and how photographers, filmmakers, and painters use color to share their views of the world. As you explore, use your Science Log to record some ways that you might use color in your artwork to share your view of the world.

1 LIGHT YOU CAN SEE

Perhaps you've walked home from school after a rainstorm and spotted a rainbow. In this lesson, you'll discover how sunlight is changed into a colorful rainbow.

A C T I V I T Y

What Color Is White Light?

Is white light white? Explore white light with a prism to find out.

DO THIS

❶ Work with a partner. Fill the bottle two-thirds full of water. One partner squeezes the bottle to force the air out. The other partner tightens the bottle cap.

❷ Pinch one side of the bottle out as you push the other side down flat against the tabletop. Try to mold the bottle into a triangular shape.

❸ Place two pieces of duct tape across the flashlight lens to make a narrow (2-mm) slit.

❹ Darken the room and shine the flashlight onto the wall. What do you see?

❺ Now shine the light through different areas of your prism. Project the light on the wall. What do you see?

THINK AND WRITE

1. How did you turn your prism to get the best rainbows?

2. Were the colors always in the same order?

How Are Rainbows Formed?

There's something about rainbows that has inspired works of art and tales of fantasy. But what really causes a rainbow to form in the sky? This poem gives one person's view.

How Gray the Rain

by Elizabeth Coatsworth

How gray the rain
And gray the world
And gray the rain clouds overhead,
When suddenly
Some cloud is furled
And there is gleaming sun instead!

The raindrops drip
Prismatic light,
And trees and meadows burn
*   in green,*
And arched in air
Serene and bright
The rainbow all at once is seen.

Serene and bright
The rainbow stands
That was not anywhere before,
And so may joy
Fill empty hands
When someone enters
*   through a door.*

Rainbows are formed when the white light of the sun passes through raindrops. Each raindrop acts like a *prism*. The raindrop refracts, or bends, the light into the individual colors that make up the white light. These colors are the colors of the *visible spectrum,* the range of colors humans can see. Each color of the visible spectrum is refracted by a different amount. Red is refracted the most, followed by orange, yellow, green, blue, and finally violet, which is refracted the least. This series of refractions is what creates the bands of color that form a rainbow when the sun peeks through the clouds on a rainy day.

You may wish to write a poem about rainbows. Include in your poem at least one fact you have learned about rainbows.

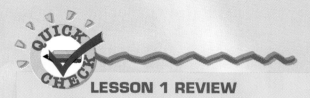

LESSON 1 REVIEW

Draw a ray diagram to show how white light is refracted through a prism. Include and label a different ray for each color of the visible spectrum.

2 BUILDING WITH COLORS

On a color TV screen, tiny bars of red, blue, and green combine to form all the brilliant colors you see as you watch a show. On these pages, you'll see how colors are created.

A C T I V I T Y

A Colored-Light Show

How do three colors combine to produce all the colors you see on TV? Do this activity to find out.

DO THIS

1 Cover the lens of each flashlight with a different color of cellophane, and secure the cellophane with tape.

2 In a darkened classroom, shine one flashlight at a time onto the white paper. Record what color you see.

3 Shine the flashlights in combinations of two and three so the rays of light overlap on the paper. Make a chart to show the color each combination produces.

THINK AND WRITE

Describe how you would use primary-color filters on your flashlights to create special effects for a show.

Building Colors The colors of the tiny bars on a TV screen and the colored light beams of your flashlights are *primary light* colors. The colors created by combining primary light colors are *secondary light* colors.

ACTIVITY

Food-Color Kaleidoscope

Try this activity to see how products found in many kitchens and bakeries can be used to make a kaleidoscope of color.

DO THIS

1 Cover the bottom of the petri dish with 1 cm of milk.

2 Drip one drop of each food coloring onto the milk. The drops should be placed around the edge of the dish and should form the points of a square.

3 Place a drop of detergent in the center of the dish.

4 Observe the milk until the color movement stops. Record your observations.

5 Stir the colors together.

MATERIALS

- petri dish
- whole milk
- red, yellow, blue, and green food coloring
- liquid dish detergent
- dropper
- spoon
- Science Log data sheet

THINK AND WRITE

1. What new colors were made while the colors moved? What color did you observe after you stirred the colors together?

2. Why would it be helpful to know how to combine different-colored liquids to make new colors?

Testing Color Vision

You've explored how some colors are produced. Now it's time to investigate how your eyes see the colors around you.

MATERIALS
- meter stick
- several different-colored pieces of paper (each about 10 cm square)
- Science Log data sheet

DO THIS

1 One group member sits in a chair and looks straight ahead. A second group member holds the meter stick as shown. The zero mark should be beside an ear of the seated student.

2 Another student selects one of the pieces of colored paper. This student holds the paper alongside the meter stick. Next, this student moves the piece of paper along the meter stick until the seated student identifies the color. Record the point on the meter stick at which the student recognizes the color. Repeat this step for each color.

3 Repeat the experiment with another group member seated in the chair. Compare and discuss the results in your group and with other groups.

THINK AND WRITE

COMPARING You compared the distances at which each student could first see different colors through his or her peripheral vision. (*Peripheral* means "at the edges.") According to your comparison, was one color seen sooner—more easily—than the others? Explain.

How Do We See Color?

In Section A, you discovered some of the similarities between the lenses of your eyes and the lens of a camera. As you follow the path an image takes through a color TV camera and TV set to you, look for other similarities between TV equipment and your eyes.

What you see on a color TV set starts with an image. Prisms inside a color TV camera refract the light from the image in front of it into the primary light colors: red, green, and blue. Three camera tubes, one for each color, produce signals that communicate the image's color and brightness.

These signals are received by antennas or satellite dishes and are then broadcast to the receiver on a color TV. These signals carry all the information needed so the TV set can reproduce the image and the sound recorded by the camera. The TV receiver sends the signal to the TV picture tube.

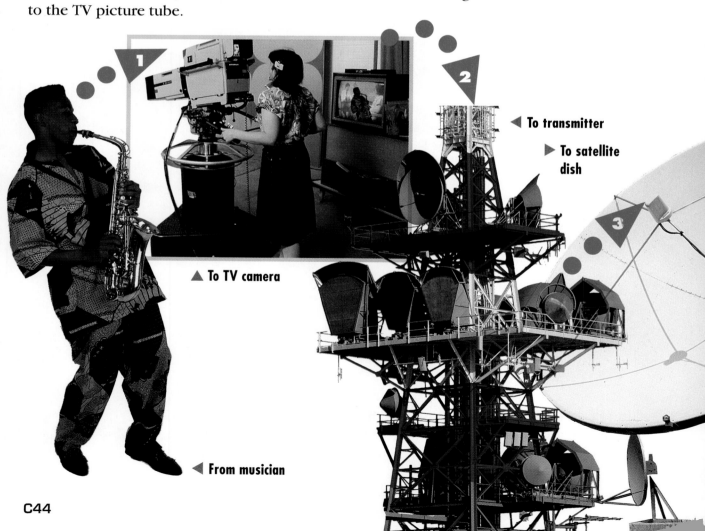

◀ To transmitter

▶ To satellite dish

▲ To TV camera

◀ From musician

The picture tube sends signals to the screen. The combination of color bars in red, green, and blue reproduces the original image in all of its many colors and degrees of brightness.

The color image is then reflected from the TV screen to your eyes. In each eye, the image passes through your pupil and lens and onto your retina.

When light hits your retina, two kinds of cells—rods and cones— are stimulated. *Rods* are not sensitive to color, but they help you see in very dim light. *Cones*, which are sensitive to color, need good light to work. There are three types of cones, each type sensitive to either red, green, or blue light. Cones work together to send information about the image's colors through your optic nerve.

The optic nerve for each of your eyes carries the information in the form of impulses to your brain. Your brain "translates" the information into a color image for you to see.

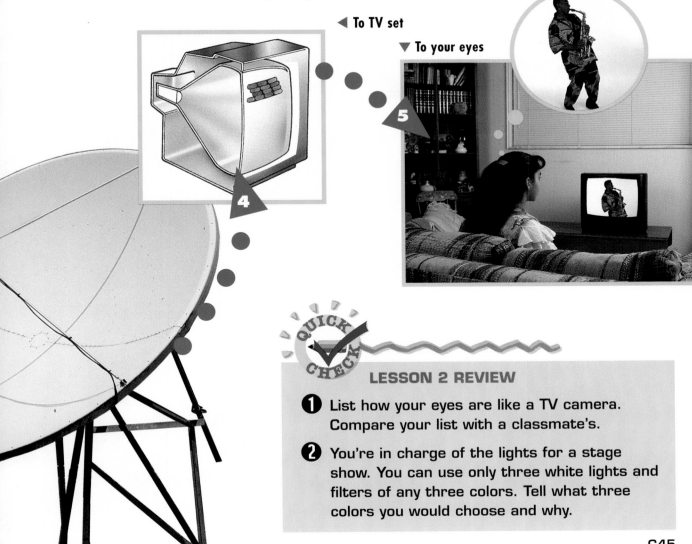

◀ To TV set

▼ To your eyes

5

4

LESSON 2 REVIEW

❶ List how your eyes are like a TV camera. Compare your list with a classmate's.

❷ You're in charge of the lights for a stage show. You can use only three white lights and filters of any three colors. Tell what three colors you would choose and why.

3 WHY OPAQUE OBJECTS HAVE COLOR

You'd probably be surprised to see a black tomato or a red cucumber. But why do things appear to have a certain color? In this lesson, you'll discover why opaque objects have colors and how their colors can appear to change.

A C T I V I T Y

By Any Other Light

Can the color of light in which an object is seen affect the color the object seems to be? Do this activity to find out.

MATERIALS
- four flashlights
- red, blue, and green cellophane
- transparent tape
- opaque object of each color: red, orange, yellow, green, blue, violet, black, and white
- Science Log data sheet

DO THIS

❶ Cover the lens of each of three flashlights with either red, blue, or green cellophane, and secure the cellophane with tape. The light from the fourth flashlight will remain white.

◀ Tomato—white light

▼ Tomato—blue light

▼ Tomato—green light

▼ Tomato—red light

C46

❷ You'll be testing the color of opaque objects as you shine different colors of light on them. Make a table like the one below on which to record your results. Title your table.

white light								
red light								
blue light								
green light								

❸ Darken the room, and shine each color of light on each object. Record the color the object appears to be each time.

THINK AND WRITE

1. When you looked at an opaque object under white light, the color you saw was the color reflected by the object. All other colors were absorbed. For each object in your table, tell under each color of light which colors were absorbed and which were reflected.

2. Why do you think a red object appears black under green light?

3. Black objects *absorb* nearly all light. White objects *reflect* nearly all light. Tell why you think it's a good idea to wear white clothes on a hot, sunny day.

4. Add a new object to your chart. Predict what color it will be under each color of light. Test your predictions.

How Artists Create Color

Look through any collection of paintings in a museum or in a book, and you'll notice a tremendous variety of colors. How do you think artists create the many different colors for their paintings?

Photo Researchers, Georges Seurat, *Sunday Afternoon on the Island of La Grande Jatte.* Art Institute of Chicago.

◀ **Sunday Afternoon on the Island of La Grande Jatte by Georges Seurat**

You've explored how red, blue, and green light can be combined to create color images for films and TV. Painters also combine colors to create new colors. But since they are working with paints, not light, they use a slightly different technique.

Paints are opaque—the colors we perceive are created by the light reflected by the paints. Each pigment, paint, and dye is made of materials that are especially good at absorbing light so that each reflects only one very specific color of light.

The *primary pigments*, like the primary colors of light, are colors that can be combined to create every other color. The primary pigments are yellow, magenta, and cyan.

Mixing pigments in different combinations will change the colors of light that are absorbed and reflected. That's why mixing pigments makes it possible to create thousands of different colors.

THINK ABOUT IT

Look at the notes you made when you overlapped primary colors of light. Do you think there is a relationship between the secondary light colors and the primary pigments? Explain.

ACTIVITY

Experimenting with Pigments

MATERIALS
• yellow, magenta, and cyan paints
• spoons
• small paper cups
• paintbrushes
• poster board
• Science Log data sheet

Painters must learn how to mix paints to create colors that are just right for their projects. Try your hand at mixing colors as you create some artwork.

DO THIS

1 Choose something you would like to create with paints.

2 Make a table like the one shown to record colors you might want to use for your project.

Possible Colors for my Project	
Colors Combined	Results
1 part cyan 1 part yellow	

3 Use a spoon to measure equal parts of two of the primary pigments, and mix them in a cup. Record your results on your table. Repeat the procedure, mixing equal parts of each possible combination of two primary pigments. Then combine equal parts of all three pigments. Record your results.

4 Continue experimenting with different proportions of primary pigments. Record your results.

5 Select appropriate colors and complete your art project.

THINK AND WRITE

How many different colors were you able to create from just three pigments?

LESSON 3 REVIEW

Mixing the three primary pigment colors in equal parts creates black. Explain why.

DOUBLE CHECK

SECTION B REVIEW

1. How are the primary colors of light and the primary pigments alike? How are they different?

2. Why do you think many people wear black or other dark-colored clothing during winter to keep themselves warmer?

Sound Check!

▶ **Tuning forks**

Think of a concert you have attended or seen on TV. Lighting and special effects might have made it more exciting to watch, but listening to the music was probably more important to you. Sound effects in movies and TV shows often set the mood for the story. Just listen—sounds are all around you.

In this section, you'll explore some of the characteristics of sound and have a chance to create sounds of your own. What characteristics of sound are important to consider when preparing for and performing in a concert? In your Science Log, describe how sounds are produced and controlled during a concert.

1 TUNING IN TO SOUND

You're listening to a recording of your favorite group. You turn up the volume and begin to sing along. How are music and other sounds produced? How does sound travel? You'll find answers to these questions in this lesson.

Sound Out

Take some time to think about how sound is a part of your world. Here are some ideas to get you started.

Keep a Sound Log

Carry your Science Log with you for at least a day, and write down the sounds that you hear. Compare your list to a classmate's. Discuss what or who made each sound. Were you surprised at any of the sounds you heard? Do you think people living 200 years ago would have had the same list of sounds? Explain.

Write a Sound Poem

Buzz, crackle, clang, and *zap* are examples of words that sound like what they are describing. Writers use words like these to help readers "hear" the sounds being described. Make a list of words that describe sounds you hear during your day. Use those words in a poem.

Talk About Sound

Ask family members to describe one sound that they think is unpleasant and one sound they think is pleasant. Did you all have the same opinions about sounds? Explain your answer.

▲ Sound is all around.

THINK ABOUT IT

What are some other ways you can tune in to sounds?

ACTIVITY

What Happens When a Sound Is Made?

Hearing is one way of experiencing sounds. But you can also feel and see the effects of sounds. In this activity, what you see and feel will help you form a hypothesis about sounds.

MATERIALS

- coffee can
- plastic wrap
- rubber band
- salt
- pencil with eraser
- radio
- Science Log data sheet

DO THIS

1 Make a drum by stretching a piece of plastic wrap across the open end of an empty coffee can. Use the rubber band to hold the wrap tightly in place. Sprinkle a small amount of salt on top of the plastic wrap.

2 Gently tap the metal bottom of the coffee can with the eraser end of a pencil. What do you observe?

3 Now gently strike the plastic wrap, as if you were playing a drum. What do you observe now?

4 Place the coffee can on the radio, and turn the volume up. Observe the salt on the plastic wrap. Place your hands on the radio while the volume is turned up. What do you feel now?

5 Place your fingers gently on your throat while you hum a tune or say a few words. What do you feel?

THINK AND WRITE

HYPOTHESIZING You form a hypothesis to explain how or why something happens. Make a list of what you saw or felt for each sound you heard. Use your observations to write a hypothesis to explain how sounds are produced and transmitted.

Make a Telephone

Of all the sounds you hear throughout the day, the most common just might be a human voice. As you explore one way you can hear a voice, keep in mind the hypothesis you wrote after the last activity. See if your hypothesis is supported by what you discover.

DO THIS

1. Use a pencil point to make a small hole in the center of the bottom of two paper cups.

2. Insert one end of a piece of string through the hole from the outside of one cup. Tie a paper clip onto the end of the string, and pull the clip and excess string back into the cup. Repeat this process with the other end of the string and another cup.

3. Hold one cup and give the other cup to a partner. Move apart until the string is stretched tight.

4. Talk into your cup while your partner holds the other cup over his or her ear. Take turns talking and listening through the paper-cup telephones. Try whispering. How well can you hear each other? Gently touch the string while you are talking. What do you feel?

5. Make new paper-cup telephones with lines made of yarn and of fishing line. Repeat steps 3 and 4.

6. Repeat steps 1–5, using the foam cups.

THINK AND WRITE

Compare the quality of sound you heard over each telephone. Which cup and telephone line were the best transmitters of sound?

Listening to Underwater Sounds

Most of the sounds you hear probably travel through air or solids. This passage tells about an animal that depends on its keen ability to hear underwater. Read the passage, and then do the next activity. Think about why dolphins and other whales depend on hearing, rather than sight, in their lives underwater.

Dolphins: Our Friends in the Sea

from *Dolphins: Our Friends in the Sea*
by **Judith E. Rinard**

LITERATURE In whales, hearing is the most highly developed sense. It helps them communicate, navigate, and find food in the ocean. They use a system of sound waves called echolocation. The dolphin's brain shows the greatest development in the areas devoted to hearing.

To echolocate, dolphins send out high-pitched clicking sounds—as many as 1,200 a second. The clicks may be seven to eight times higher than sounds humans can hear.

As a dolphin swims through the water, it moves its head back and forth to scan for objects ahead. When the clicking sounds hit an object, such as a rock or a fish, the sounds bounce back as echoes. Scientists hypothesize that these echoes travel through the dolphin's lower jaw to the inner ear.

▲ Above water, dolphins make sounds through air cavities.

Then they are transmitted to the brain. Much like a computer, the brain analyzes the echoes and tells the dolphin the location, size, and shape of the object.

In experiments designed to test the dolphin's ability to echolocate, scientists have found that a blindfolded dolphin can tell the difference between a dime and a nickel when both are thrown into the dolphin's pool!

THINK ABOUT IT

Describe any times when you have heard sounds underwater or when you have heard your voice echo, or bounce back to you.

The Medium Matters

Which is a better medium for carrying sound—air or water?
Do this activity to find out.

DO THIS

1 Work with a partner. Fill two balloons with water. Tie each closed with a piece of string. Take a balloon, and stand across the room from your partner.

2 Ask another student to strike a coat hanger with a wooden dowel. Describe what you hear.

MATERIALS
- several balloons
- water
- string
- 1 metal coat hanger
- wooden dowel
- Science Log data sheet

3 Extend a long string between your water balloon and your partner's balloon as you hold your balloons against your ears. The string should be fairly taut.

4 Have the third person hang the coat hanger on the string and strike it again. Have someone move the coat hanger to different parts of the string, and listen to how the sound changes when the coat hanger is struck. Record your observations.

5 Repeat steps 2 through 4 with balloons filled with air.

THINK AND WRITE

Does sound travel better in water or in air? Explain.

Taking a Closer Look at Sound

As you've discovered, every day you hear many different sounds from many different sources. But, as you will read below, all of the sounds you hear have one thing in common. Not sure what that thing is? Here's a hint: Think about what a guitar string does after it is plucked.

Sound waves are formed by an object's **vibrations**. The vibrations cause the molecules around the object to first press closer together and then to separate—again and again. This is like the action of pushing a long coiled spring forward, compressing the coils, and then pulling back, separating the coils. The energy of a vibration moves through the medium around an object in the same way as it moves down the length of the coiled spring.

The sound from a vibrating drumhead spreads outward in all directions. The pressure waves, formed by the compressing and separating of the air molecules, are like ever-enlarging spheres coming from the sound source at the center. The distance between two waves is one **wavelength**. As each wave moves outward, its energy is spread out more thinly. This is why a sound becomes softer as you move farther away from the source. The **frequency** of a sound tells how often a wave is produced.

Sound waves can travel through liquids, gases, or solids. In Section A, you read that light changed speed when it passed from one medium to another. A change in medium affects the speed of sound waves, too.

At sea level, sound travels through air at about 340 meters (1,115 feet) per second.

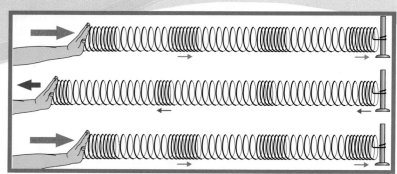

▲ Sound waves, like coils in a spring, move back and forth.

▲ Sound waves spread outward in circles.

▲ Sound travels through water, a liquid.

Sound travels through water at about 1,500 meters (4,921 feet) per second.

Sound travels through wood at about 3,800 meters (12,467 feet) per second. Denser materials, such as steel, carry sound even faster, at more than 5,000 meters (16,404 feet) per second.

Why do you think sound travels faster in solids than in liquids or gases? Here's a hint: In a solid, the molecules are closer together than they are in a gas or a liquid. Now think again about why the type of medium affects the speed at which sound travels.

▲ Sound travels through air, a gas.

▲ Sound travels through wood, a solid.

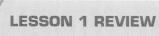

LESSON 1 REVIEW

Explain in your own words how sound is produced and how it travels.

2 HOW WE HEAR SOUND

Have you ever cupped your hand to your ear to help you hear a faint sound? If so, you've already discovered the first step in the path a sound takes on the way to being heard by you. Read on to find out more.

The Ears Have It

Have you ever thought about why your ears are shaped as they are? How are your ears different from the ears of other animals?

▲ Cupping an ear helps gather sound waves.

▼ Some animals, such as deer, dogs, and bats, can move their ears to help gather sound waves.

The curves and ridges of the human ear serve an important purpose. They collect the sound waves that travel into your ear.

Many animals have ears adapted to collect sound waves, too. Compare the animal ears pictured and your own. Why do you think it would be an advantage to have large ears that can move and turn?

Once the sound is collected by the outer ear, a chain of events enables you to hear the waves in the form of a sound. Look at the diagram to see what happens.

Listen to the sounds around you. Now try covering your ears with your hands. You can still hear some sound, although perhaps less clearly. Why? Sound waves hitting your skull cause it to vibrate. These vibrations cause the cochlea to vibrate, and the process continues as if the sound waves had entered through the ear.

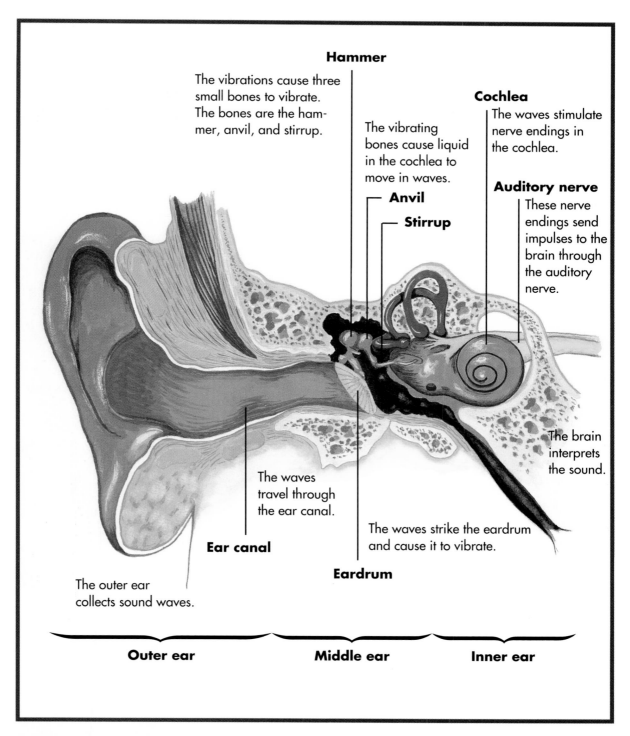

Hammer

The vibrations cause three small bones to vibrate. The bones are the hammer, anvil, and stirrup.

The vibrating bones cause liquid in the cochlea to move in waves.

Cochlea
The waves stimulate nerve endings in the cochlea.

Anvil

Stirrup

Auditory nerve
These nerve endings send impulses to the brain through the auditory nerve.

The waves travel through the ear canal.

Ear canal

The waves strike the eardrum and cause it to vibrate.

Eardrum

The brain interprets the sound.

The outer ear collects sound waves.

Outer ear   Middle ear   Inner ear

THINK ABOUT IT

Why do you think it is helpful to have an ear on each side of your head? Discuss with a partner some of the advantages and disadvantages of the placement and shape of human ears.

Hearing in Different Ways

The passage below is from a book about Amy Rowley, who has been hearing-impaired since birth. As you read, look for devices and skills Amy uses to communicate with hearing people.

Amy: THE STORY OF A DEAF CHILD

by **Lou Ann Walker,** with photographs by **Michael Abramson**

I love to climb trees. I also like to take care of my pets—my rabbit Brown Eyes, my cat Checkers, and my parakeet Garfield. Also my fish. If you look closely at this picture, you can see my hearing aid. My mom and dad are deaf, too. My brother John is hearing. He's thirteen. I'm eleven.

In the mornings, my alarm clock has a flashing light to wake me up. I like it better when my mom comes to get me out of bed.

▲ Amy with a "friend"

▲ Amy's body aid helps her understand another student.

Our house also has lights that flash when someone rings the doorbell.

I can hear myself talking right now. I can hear some sounds, but I can't understand everything. Say I heard an ambulance go by. I wouldn't know what it was unless I saw it.

All the other kids who go to my school are hearing. I'm the only deaf person at Furnace Woods School.

When I'm in school, I wear a body aid: a big hearing aid that fits on my belt. My teachers wear microphones that send signals to the body aid.

Reading lips helps me understand what people are saying. But I can't really understand the noises I hear from my body aid without looking at people's mouths.

If I can't figure out what the teacher is saying, I ask "What?" Then he repeats it, and I look closer at his mouth. I probably say "What?" more than most people do, but I want to know everything that is going on. Sometimes kids don't understand what I say, and so I have to repeat myself, too.

Some people shout at me. They think I'll be able to hear them better. It's harder to understand them, though, because shouting makes their mouths look strange so that I can't even lip-read.

▲ **Amy and a friend are finger-spelling.**

Lots of hearing people ask me what it's like to be deaf, but I never ask them what it's like to be hearing.

I think deafness feels like peace. Hearing people have to hear all sorts of things they don't want to hear. I don't.

QUICK CHECK

LESSON 2 REVIEW

❶ Suppose Amy is coming to your school. What can be done to make sure Amy is able to attend the same classes and do the same activities as hearing people?

❷ How can a person who can't hear make up for the impairment by using his or her other senses? Make a list of your ideas.

❸ List three new things you have learned about hearing.

3 COMPARING SOUNDS

You've discovered that all sounds have one thing in common: They are caused by vibrations that form sound waves. But all sounds don't sound the same, do they? As you do the activity and read the information on this and the following pages, look for ways to describe the sounds you most like to hear.

ACTIVITY

Make Your Own Music

You don't need to buy a musical instrument to create sound. All you need are a few ordinary objects and a little bit of creativity. Try it!

DO THIS

1 Make a table to keep track of each sound you discover and to tell how it is made. On your table, record any observations you make about the sound and its characteristics. The next page shows one way you might organize your data.

2 Work in a group to make a variety of sounds, using your materials. Combine materials to make musical instruments. Strike different objects with spoons. Strike gently if the object is glass. Instruments you've seen, such as drums or guitars, might give you some ideas. Try to invent new ways of making sound, too.

MATERIALS

collection of readily available objects, such as

- plastic and metal containers with lids
- marbles
- cardboard boxes
- plastic wrap and wax paper
- rubber bands of different sizes
- pieces of wood
- drinking straws
- string or fishing line
- glass bottles filled with water
- metal and plastic pipes
- wooden, metal, and plastic spoons
- Science Log data sheet

Materials	What We Did	Observations
wood blocks rubber bands and shoe box		

3 As you make your observations, consider the following questions:

- Is the sound loud or soft?
- Which materials make the highest sounds?
- What can you do to change a sound without changing the materials used?

THINK AND WRITE

1. What, of anything you tried, made a sound you could barely hear? Why do you think that happened?

2. What variables affect the characteristics of a sound?

3. **COMPARING** Comparing provides you with an opportunity to determine the characteristics of each instrument in the activity. Describe how you determined which instrument made the highest sound.

Qualities of Sound

A TV show or a concert wouldn't be very interesting if it weren't for the great variety of the sounds that we can hear. As you read, look for ways to describe the sounds you created in the last activity.

▲ Tuba

◀ School band

▲ Flute

Sounds can be described as having pitch and volume. *Pitch* describes how high or low a sound is. *Volume* describes how loud or soft a sound is. First let's take a closer look at pitch.

You've discovered that a sound is made by vibrations. Think about how a guitar string vibrates when it is plucked. The speed of the string's vibration, or its *frequency*, affects the pitch. Frequency is measured in number of vibrations per second, or *hertz*. Humans hear sounds ranging from about 20 hertz (a very low pitch) to 20,000 hertz (a very high pitch).

A tuba has a lower pitch than a flute. A violin has a higher pitch than a bass. Think about the instruments you made in the last activity. Which instrument had the lowest pitch? Which had the highest pitch?

Pitch is affected by the amount of matter that is vibrating. In stringed musical instruments, a longer or thicker string has a lower pitch than a shorter or thinner string. In wind instruments, a larger column of air produces a lower pitch than a smaller column of air. The more material there is to vibrate, the lower the pitch will be.

▲ Bass

▶ Violin

Tension affects pitch, too. A tighter string produces a higher pitch than a looser string.

Most musical instruments can play a range of pitches. These pitches are called tones. Tones form a musical scale, and a scale with eight tones is called an *octave*.

The letters on this staff represent the tones in one octave. The pitch of the tones gets higher as you move up the scale.

Pitch isn't the only thing that affects how something sounds. Use your hand to strike a table or desk gently. Now use the same part of your hand to strike the table harder. You haven't changed the pitch of the sound, but you have changed the volume.

When you hit the table the second time, you used more energy and increased the sound's volume. A sound's volume is measured in *decibels*.

Sounds that are louder than 100 decibels can permanently damage your ears. Many construction and factory workers and people working on airport runways must wear ear protectors. Listening to any sound at a high volume, such as music or noise from a TV, can damage your ears if you do it over a long period of time.

▼ TV, 60 decibels or more

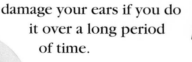

▲ A whisper, 20 decibels

▲ Jet airplane,
140 decibels

QUICK CHECK

LESSON 3 REVIEW

❶ What is the difference between pitch and volume?

❷ How can a sound's pitch and volume be changed?

C65

4 CONTROLLING SOUND

Have you ever been told to turn down loud music at home?
Have you ever had trouble hearing a speaker in an auditorium?
As you read, think about times that sound volume needs to be controlled.

ACTIVITY
Throwing Your Voice

Sound engineers can control sound in many ways. In this activity, you will become a sound engineer by directing sound.

MATERIALS
- 2 umbrellas
- aluminum foil
- Science Log data sheet

DO THIS

1 Stand back-to-back with a partner.

2 Hold an open umbrella to one side. Talk in a normal voice as you slowly move the umbrella until it is in front of your face. Ask your partner to listen for any changes in the way your voice sounds. Can your partner guess when the umbrella is directly in front of your face?

3 Give your partner the other umbrella. Stand back-to-back again, and hold your umbrellas in front of your faces. Speak again while your partner listens. Can your partner tell the difference between your voice now and when there was just one umbrella?

4 Line the inside of the umbrellas with foil and try steps 2 and 3 again. Can you notice a difference in the sound?

THINK AND WRITE

Draw diagrams to show how the sound waves traveled in steps 2 and 3. Use your diagrams to explain the difference made by the second umbrella. What effect did the foil have?

Testing for Sound

If your favorite band came to your school, where would its music sound the best? Do this activity to find out.

DO THIS

1 Describe each room. How large is it? What materials are on the floor, ceiling, windows, and walls? What kind of furniture is there?

2 In each room, place the tape player on the floor. Always play the same song at the same volume.

3 Listen from several locations within the room. Describe how the music sounds. Can you hear echoes?

MATERIALS
- several rooms in your school
- tape player and music tape of your choice
- Science Log data sheet

THINK AND WRITE

In which room did the music sound best? What conditions in that room might have helped make it a good room for listening to music?

Sounding Good

In the last activity, you identified rooms that were good places to listen to music. Now read to find out why sound carries better in some rooms than in others.

Acoustics is the science of sound. One important application of acoustics is in the design of buildings.

You've discovered that sound is produced by vibrations that form waves. Understanding how the sound waves can be reflected or absorbed is important to a knowledge of acoustics.

For a place like a concert hall or an auditorium, "good acoustics" would mean that music or other sounds can be heard clearly anywhere in the room. The shape of an auditorium is important for good acoustics. A curved ceiling, for example, can help reflect sound waves from the stage to the audience. Acoustics can even be affected in an outdoor performance area. How do you think the backdrop of the outdoor theater shown on the next page reflects sound?

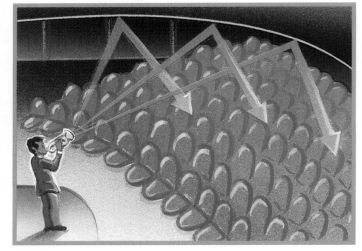

Sometimes you hear echoes when sound is reflected. *Echoes* are reflected sound waves. They occur when sound waves are reflected from a distant source, like the wall of a canyon. If a sound is reflected from several different points, you hear *reverberation,* a quick series of echoes.

Sometimes rooms are designed to absorb sound instead of reflecting it. Soft materials, like carpets and drapes, help absorb sound waves. Acoustical tile, a soft tile with tiny holes in it, is used in ceilings and walls of recording studios and other places where people do not want sound to be reflected.

Factories often need to soundproof areas where noisy machinery is used. Walls, floors, and ceilings are constructed with materials that absorb sound so that the noise does not travel to other parts of the building.

Acoustics are important in homes, too. Carpeting and insulated walls can help keep sound from traveling from one room to another.

▲ Hollywood Bowl

▲ Food court

▲ Printing press

▲ Recording studio

▲ Canyon

▲ Home

▲ Library

QUICK CHECK

LESSON 4 REVIEW

Design a recording studio for your school, and tell what materials you would use to build it.

 DOUBLE CHECK

SECTION C REVIEW

Think of a concert you have attended or of a place where you have listened to music. Describe how different instruments produced sound. Tell about the acoustics of the site.

Switch It On!

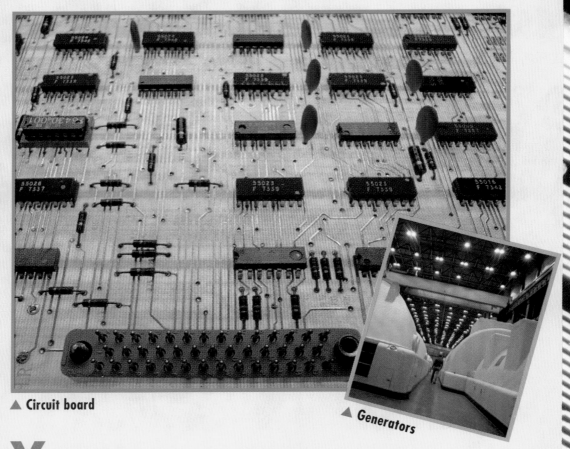

▲ Circuit board

▲ Generators

You've seen how light and sound each play a role in the creation and recording of much of what you see in a live performance or on TV. But there's one key ingredient that helps bring it all together: electricity.

How is electricity used in creating, recording, and transmitting stage performances? As you explore ways that electricity can be controlled, research ways in which electronics is used to create music. Describe types of musical performances that depend on electronic sound. Record the results of your research in your Science Log.

1 LET THE CURRENT FLOW

How does electricity "know" where to go when you plug in an electric guitar and switch it on? In this lesson, you will discover how the flow of electricity is controlled.

The Electronic Stage

You may have enjoyed a concert like this one in person or on TV. Now take a look at the equipment that uses electricity during the show.

Sounds from the electric guitar can be amplified so they are heard throughout the auditorium. The microphone turns the singer's voice into electronic impulses that can be amplified and recorded. Electronic synthesizers can produce any sound you can think of. Speakers amplify and direct the sounds.

Backstage, an engineer uses an electronic soundboard to control the volume and balance of the sounds. Even if you miss the show, you can enjoy it later. Video and sound equipment can record the show for broadcast.

THINK ABOUT IT

How is electricity used during a concert?

ACTIVITY

Your Own Circuit

You began your investigations in this unit by wondering about what goes into staging and recording a musical performance. Do this activity to investigate how electronic equipment really works.

DO THIS

1 Work with the bulb, battery, and wires until you get the bulb to light. Draw a picture to show exactly how you arranged the materials to turn on the light.

2 Connect the materials to light the bulb in as many other ways as possible.

THINK AND WRITE

1. Draw a diagram to represent each of your arrangements. Use the symbols for the battery, wire, and light as shown on the diagram below.

2. Look at your diagrams. Compare your successful and unsuccessful attempts to light the bulb. What was needed to produce a successful circuit?

MATERIALS
- light bulb and holder
- battery
- battery holder
- 3 10-cm pieces of insulated wire, with 1-cm of bare wire on each end
- Science Log data sheet

Simple Circuit Each time you arranged your materials to light the bulb, you created an electric circuit. An **electric circuit** is a closed pathway for electricity to follow. Scientists use circuit diagrams like this one to show what is happening in an electric circuit.

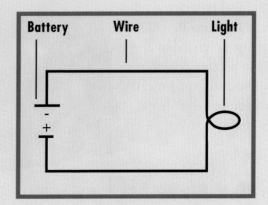

A Water Circuit

What images come to mind when you think of current flowing through an electric circuit? Since you can't see electric current, take a moment to think about a circuit you can see. Look for similarities between the water circuit described and the electric circuits you created.

▼ The pump rotates, creating a pressure difference to drive the water. A stronger pump would push the water through faster.

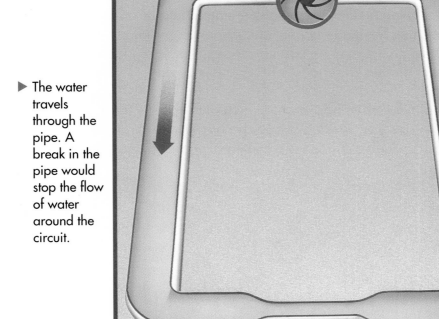

► The water travels through the pipe. A break in the pipe would stop the flow of water around the circuit.

◄ The water returns to the pump, and the cycle continues.

▲ The narrowed pipe slows the flow of water passing through the pipe.

THINK ABOUT IT

Compare the water circuit described above with the electric circuits you made. Which parts of an electric circuit function like the water pump and pipe? Which part of an electric circuit would affect the flow of current, just as the narrowed water pipe slows the flow of water?

▶ A battery's negative terminal has more negative charges than positive charges.

▲ A battery's positive terminal has more positive charges than negative charges.

What Is an Electric Circuit?

Whether you are using electricity to light a single bulb or to fill an auditorium with sights and sounds, the principles of electric circuits remain the same. As you continue to explore electric circuits, keep in mind the model of the water circuit.

Resistance is a measure of how much a material opposes the flow of electricity. The wire inside the light bulb resists the flow of electricity. The resistance causes the filament to heat up and glow.

Current is the flow of negatively charged atomic particles called *electrons*.

THINK ABOUT IT

Why does an electric light bulb glow?

◀ An electric circuit is the path from one terminal to the other along which electricity flows.

▶ Wire provides the pathway along which electrons flow from the negative terminal to the positive terminal.

How Strong Are Your Batteries?

Earlier in this section, you used a battery to light a light bulb. In this activity, you'll explore ways to increase the amount of energy in a system.

MATERIALS
- 4 batteries
- 4 battery holders
- 2 10-cm pieces of insulated wire, with 1 cm of bare wire on each end
- light bulb and holder
- Science Log data sheet

DO THIS

1 Make a circuit by using one battery, the wire, and the bulb. Observe the brightness of the light.

2 Add a second battery to your circuit by placing the positive end of one battery against the negative end of the other battery. Observe the brightness of the light. How does it compare with the light produced by one battery?

3 Repeat step 2, adding a third and then a fourth battery.

THINK AND WRITE

1. Describe the relationship between the number of batteries and the brightness of the bulb.

2. EXPERIMENTING When you experiment in an activity, you are comparing the effects of variables. How might your experiment have been affected if you had used two light bulbs?

ⒶⒸⓉⒾⓋⒾⓉⓎ

Conductor or Insulator?

Can the materials used in an electric circuit affect the flow of electric current? As you do this activity, think about when it might be useful to prevent the flow of current altogether.

DO THIS

❶ Make a table with the headings *Conductors* and *Insulators*.

❷ Put the bulb, the battery, and two pieces of the wire together so that the bulb lights.

❸ Add a third piece of wire to your circuit. One end of two of the wires should not be attached to anything. When you touch the two unattached ends of wires together, your bulb should light.

MATERIALS
- light bulb and holder
- battery and holder
- 3 10-cm pieces of insulated wire, with 1 cm of bare wire on each end
- a collection of materials such as paper cups, nails, screws, toothpicks, plastic and metal spoons, rubber erasers, and cloth
- Science Log data sheet

❹ Look over your collection of materials. Predict which items will make the bulb light when the item is touched by the loose ends of the two wires.

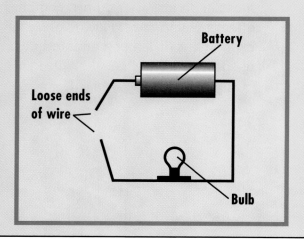

Battery

Loose ends of wire

Bulb

5 Choose one item from your collection of materials. Place the free end of each wire 1 cm apart on the material. If the bulb lights, write the name of the item under the column heading *Conductors*. If the bulb does not light, write the name of the item under the column heading *Insulators*. Repeat this step for each of the materials you collected, and record the results in your table.

THINK AND WRITE

1. Based on your observations, define the terms *conductor* and *insulator*.

2. Describe one way you might use an insulator in an electric circuit.

Superconductors Materials that allow electricity to pass through them are called *conductors*. Materials through which electricity will not pass are *insulators*.

Some materials, such as tin and lead, allow electricity to pass very easily when they are cooled to a very low temperature. When this happens, such a material becomes a *superconductor*. Superconductors can carry more electricity faster and farther. They can be used to make faster computers and more efficient motors.

The Amazing Tesla

Electric appliances require a great deal of electricity. Read about the man who made this widespread use of electricity possible.

REDISCOVERING TESLA

by **Bill Lawren** from *Omni*

Nikola Tesla insisted on having exactly 18 napkins before him at every dinner, regardless of the number of guests, and would not stay in the same room with a woman wearing pearl earrings. His startling lab demonstrations were considered better entertainment than an evening at the theater.

But there was a good deal more to Tesla than parlor magic. By 1898 he had already created two inventions that would change the world: alternating current, which made the widespread distribution of electricity possible; and the high frequency coil, which helped lay the groundwork for every broadcasting system from radio to radar. His radical and imaginative thinking foreshadowed and, to some degree, provided the conceptual basis for a remarkable variety of modern technologies.

By the middle of this century, however, Tesla had been all but forgotten. Many of his inventions were attributed to others, and his ideas were often dismissed as the ramblings of a madman. Now, Tesla and his more futuristic ideas are enjoying a revival. His work has been taken up by a new generation of inventors, researchers, and tinkerers. Like Tesla himself, they defy easy classification: They seem to run the gamut from hardheaded, practical engineers to wild-eyed fanatics. The range of their ideas is equally broad. They are working on everything from more efficient pumps and more powerful jet engines to the secret of time travel.

Tesla was born in 1856 in the tiny village of Smilijan, Croatia. From his childhood on, he demonstrated a fondness for outrageously ingenious ideas. As a student he dreamed of sending intercontinental mail via a huge sub-Atlantic tunnel. By age twenty-eight, he had already designed a prototype for the motor that would change the world.

In the 1800s, electricity was direct current, or DC, and was a purely local phenomenon. Without expensive generators to boost power over long distances, electricity could be

◄ Nikola Tesla

▼ Generating artificial lightning in Tesla's laboratory

transmitted only a few miles. Tesla designed a generator that produced current in alternating impulses. These could sustain high-voltage transmission over long distances. With this alternating current, or AC, system, electricity could be sent cheaply anywhere wires could be strung.

After a brief and stormy partnership with Thomas Edison, Tesla enlisted the support of industrialist George Westinghouse to develop a model for his AC system that revolutionized the use of electricity. He later developed the "Tesla Coils," an invention that led to the wireless transmission of electromagnetic waves: the radio.

QUICK CHECK

LESSON 1 REVIEW

1 How are conductors and insulators useful in everyday life?

2 Do you think that Tesla's characteristics helped make him a good scientist? Explain.

C79

SERIES AND PARALLEL CIRCUITS

If you were watching a concert and one of the stage lights burned out, would you expect every other piece of electronic equipment to stop working? Of course not! In this lesson, you'll explore different ways to construct an electric circuit and how to choose the best way.

ACTIVITY

Different Circuits

You've already shown how you can combine wire, a bulb, and batteries to make a bulb light. Is every circuit that lights a bulb identical? Do this activity to find out.

DO THIS

1 Make a table to record your data. Set up circuit 1 as shown. Touch both screws on the bulb holder with the wires from the voltmeter. Record the reading on the voltmeter. Remove one battery from the circuit, and record the new reading.

2 Set up circuit 2 as shown. Test the bulb with the voltmeter, and record your results. Remove one battery, test the bulb, and record your new results.

MATERIALS
- 2 batteries
- 2 battery holders
- 2 light bulbs
- 2 bulb holders
- voltmeter (0–3 V)
- 4 20-cm pieces of insulated copper wire, with 1 cm of bare wire on each end
- Science Log data sheet

3 Set up circuit 3 as shown. Test each bulb with the voltmeter. Record your results. Unscrew one of the bulbs. Test both bulbs with the voltmeter, and record your new results.

4 Set up circuit 4 as shown. Test both bulbs with the voltmeter, and record your results. Unscrew one bulb, test the remaining bulb, and record your results again.

THINK AND WRITE

1. Which circuit's bulb produced the brightest light? Which circuit's voltmeter reading was the highest? the lowest?

2. Which circuits were not affected by removing a battery? by removing a bulb?

3. Which circuit do you think has the most advantages and the fewest disadvantages?

▲ **Voltmeter**

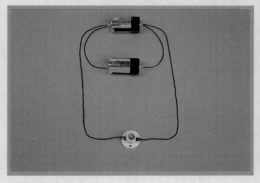

▲ **Circuit 1**

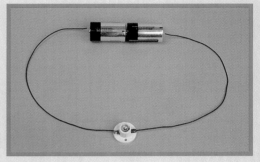

▲ **Circuit 2**

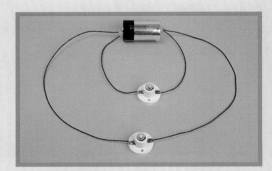

▲ **Circuit 3**

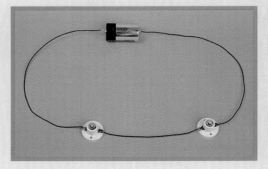

▲ **Circuit 4**

C81

Comparing Circuits

As you observed in the previous activity, the way you wire a circuit affects how it works. Take a closer look and compare two different kinds of circuits.

▼ In the circuit shown below, the current has only one path to follow. If one bulb is removed, the circuit is broken, and no bulbs will light. This is a *series circuit*.

▼ In this circuit, the current has more than one path to follow. If one bulb is removed, there is still a complete circuit to light the other bulb. This is a *parallel circuit*.

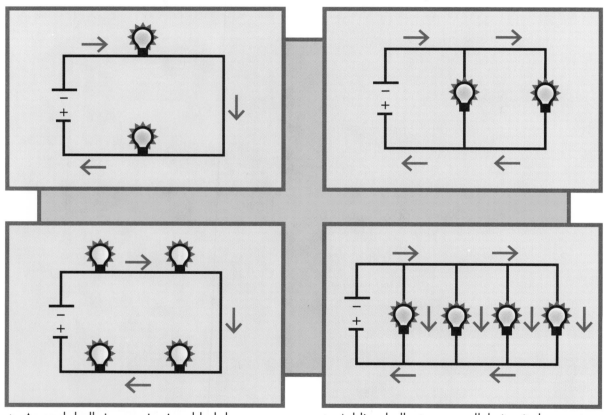

▲ As each bulb in a series is added, less energy is available to light each bulb. All the bulbs become dimmer.

▲ Adding bulbs to a parallel circuit does not affect the bulbs' brightness. Each circuit carries current to only one bulb.

THINK ABOUT IT

How would adding an extra bulb affect a series circuit? a parallel circuit? Explain.

ACTIVITY

Which Batteries Last Longer?

Have you ever discovered that your flashlight didn't work when you needed it? Has your portable radio faded out in the middle of your favorite song? Then you know the importance of helping batteries last as long as possible. In this activity, you'll use water flowing from a bottle as a model of current flowing from a battery.

MATERIALS
- 3 1-L plastic bottles
- masking tape
- water
- Science Log data sheet

DO THIS

1. Working with a partner, stick a strip of masking tape around the middle of one bottle to separate it into two halves. Then completely fill the bottle with water.

2. Fill each of the other two bottles half full of water.

3. Begin emptying one half-full bottle of water at the same time your partner begins emptying the full bottle. When your first bottle is empty, immediately begin emptying your second bottle.

THINK AND WRITE

1. Did the full bottle or the two half-full bottles empty first?

2. Which bottle or bottles could represent two batteries connected in series? in parallel?

3. **HYPOTHESIZING** When you hypothesize, you base your explanation on what you already know. Use your observations from this activity as a basis for hypothesizing which would completely use up its energy first: two batteries connected in series or two batteries connected in parallel. Describe how you could test your hypothesis.

Using the Right Circuit

You've explored the differences between series and parallel circuits. How can this understanding be applied?

Homes and offices are wired in parallel circuits. Suppose that your home were wired in a series circuit: Every appliance and light would have to be on or off at the same time. But a switch is wired in series with the appliance it controls.

▲ Parallel circuits make productions possible, allowing the producers to use a variety of multi-media equipment.

LESSON 2 REVIEW

❶ How could you determine whether a string of lights is connected in a series circuit or in a parallel circuit?

❷ Describe when and why you would use a parallel circuit.

3 CREATING WITH ELECTRONICS

Now that you understand how electricity works, you can think about how it can be used. Read this article about how one man's understanding of electricity—and his curiosity—led to one of the most common home appliances.

TV Pioneer

Today TV is common. Almost every home has a TV. Some have two or three! Your grandparents probably remember when that was not so.

PHILO FARNSWORTH: Forgotten Inventor

by Jeanne Field Olson from *Cobblestone*

 Modern television began the day young Philo Farnsworth looked back over the Idaho field he was harrowing. The pattern of the soil, shaped into rows by the harrow's disks, inspired Farnsworth's creation of the first all-electronic television system. Farnsworth believed that television could be transmitted electronically and had been trying to figure out a way to do it. Looking at the rows in the field, he realized that he could use an electron beam to scan an image line by line to turn it into an electrical pulse. That pulse could then be sent to a television receiver.

Philo Farnsworth was born in a log cabin in Utah in 1906. He was thirteen when his first invention, a "thief-proof" auto lock, won a national contest. He soon lost interest in mechanical inventions, however, and became fascinated with electricity and electrons after his family moved to Idaho, where his uncle managed a ranch that had a power plant. Philo watched the repairman who came whenever the power plant broke down and was soon able to fix it himself.

▲ **Harrowed field**

▲ **Mechanical transmission system**

A generator supplied electricity to the Farnsworths' Idaho home. Philo took apart and reassembled this generator many times. He added electric motors to his mother's hand-cranked washing machine and foot-powered sewing machine.

Farnsworth read everything he could find about electricity. He even drove a horse-drawn school wagon to earn money to buy books on the subject. Reading about early mechanical television experiments using spinning disks interested him in the idea of television. Even then he was convinced that only an all-electronic television system could succeed.

Justin Tolman, Philo's science teacher at Rigby High School in Idaho, recognized his pupil's interest and rare scientific ability and tutored him outside of class. One day after school in February 1922, fifteen-year-old Philo drew diagrams for Tolman on the school blackboards explaining his theories of an "image dissector" television camera tube and an all-electronic television system.

The next fall the Farnsworth family moved back to Utah, and Philo had to leave school. He worked at a variety of jobs from janitor to railroad electrician while taking correspondence courses in electricity and briefly attending Brigham Young University. He continued his television experiments in the college labs.

Philo met George Everson, a professional fund raiser, while both were working on a Salt Lake City Community Chest campaign. Philo was normally quiet and shy, but his enthusiasm and knowledge of electronics convinced Everson to invest six thousand dollars of his own savings in Philo's research. He also agreed to contact potential investors in California.

The conservative California bankers Everson contacted invested twenty-five thousand dollars and gave Philo Farnsworth one year to prove that his electronic camera tube could transmit a picture. He began working behind drawn blinds in a simple lab above a garage at 202 Green Street, San Francisco. His bride, Pem, learned to spot weld and helped with drafting and secretarial work.

▼ **Philo Farnsworth**

▲ First TV transmission (about 1934)

Cliff Gardner, Farnsworth's best friend and Pem's brother, was his assistant, learning glass blowing to create the special glass tubes needed.

In less than a year, Farnsworth succeeded. He was barely twenty-one when his television camera transmitted the world's first completely electronic picture on September 7, 1927. After another year's work, Farnsworth was able to transmit a much-improved picture.

THINK ABOUT IT

What made Philo Farnsworth a scientist? Describe character traits and actions he took that enabled him to realize his dream.

Putting It All Together

You've done a lot of exploring to discover how light, sound, and electricity work. Now is your chance to put your knowledge to use. Follow these guidelines for planning, recording, and sharing your own multimedia presentation.

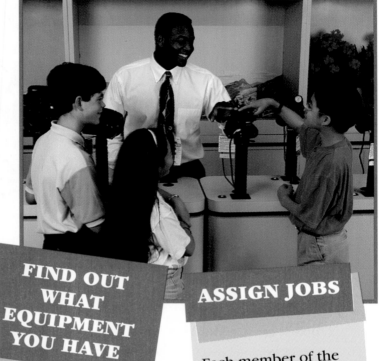

START WITH AN IDEA

Decide what kind of show you will video-tape. A concert? A music video? A play? Figure out how to use your best talents.

FIND OUT WHAT EQUIPMENT YOU HAVE

Find out what you can borrow from your school, family members, or other people in the community.

CAUTION: Find out what you need to know about using equipment safely before you begin. Ask an adult to help you with any piece of equipment that is new to you.

ASSIGN JOBS

Each member of the group should have a job to do. You'll need people to—

- write the script and plan the show.
- run the camera, lights, and any other equipment.
- perform in the show.
- plan and advertise the presentation.

GET SUPPORT

Involve people outside the school in your efforts. A local video store might lend equipment or donate supplies. Parents might help make any needed costumes or props.

KEEP A RECORD

Make a behind-the-scenes record of the process, using photographs or a video camera. Use what you've learned about sound, light, and electricity to help explain what is happening at each step.

ON WITH THE SHOW!

Share your video with as many people as possible. Show it in the school auditorium or the public library. See whether a local cable-access channel will let you broadcast your show.

QUICK CHECK

LESSON 3 REVIEW

When putting on a show, you may be a director or a camera person, but how are you a scientist?

DOUBLE CHECK

SECTION D REVIEW

Using what you learned in this section, explain how science is a part of our everyday lives. Include at least five new things you learned about light, sound, and electricity.

I REFLECT

It's time to think about the ideas you have discovered during your investigations. Think, too, about your many accomplishments.

SUMMARIZE

Answer the following in your Science Log.

1. What **I Wonder** questions have you answered in your investigations, and what new questions have you asked?

2. What have you discovered, and how have your ideas changed?

3. Did any of your discoveries surprise you? Explain.

CONNECT IDEAS

1. Describe one way in which light, sound, and electricity interact.

2. Think about the people you have read about and the experiences you have had in this unit. Tell what you think makes a good scientist.

3. How have advances in audio and visual technology affected our lives?

4. Think about the different jobs involved in planning and recording a televised event. Describe a job that interests you, and tell why you chose it.

SCIENCE PORTFOLIO

❶ Complete your Science Experiences Record.

❷ Choose several samples of your best work from each section to include in your Science Portfolio.

❸ On A Guide to My Science Portfolio, tell why you chose each sample.

I SHARE

Scientists share their discoveries and ideas and learn from one another. How can you share what you've learned?

Decide

▶ what you want to say.

▶ what the best way is to get your message across.

Share

▶ what you did and why.

▶ what worked and what didn't work.

▶ what conclusions you have drawn.

▶ what else you'd like to find out.

Find Out

▶ what classmates liked about what you shared—and why.

▶ what questions your classmates have.

SHOW OF THE YEAR!

featuring
the music of the ZipTops
comedy acts

TUESDAY MAY 10
3:00 P.M.
Parker School Auditorium

Watch us again on cable 43!
May 20 at 7:00 P.M.

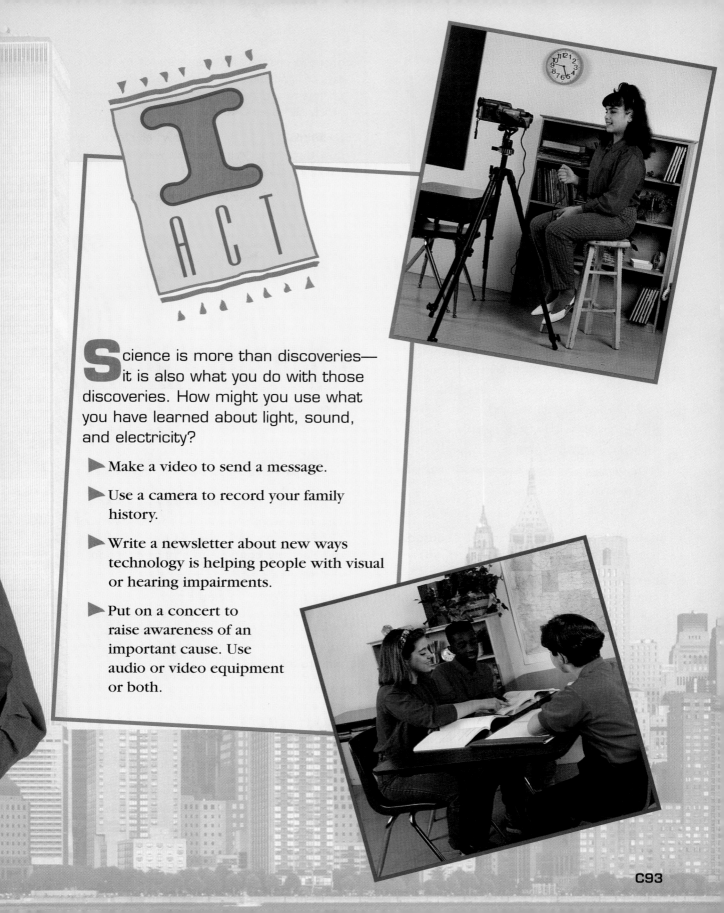

I ACT

Science is more than discoveries—it is also what you do with those discoveries. How might you use what you have learned about light, sound, and electricity?

► Make a video to send a message.

► Use a camera to record your family history.

► Write a newsletter about new ways technology is helping people with visual or hearing impairments.

► Put on a concert to raise awareness of an important cause. Use audio or video equipment or both.

THE LANGUAGE OF SCIENCE

The language of science helps people communicate clearly when they talk about light, sound, and electricity. Here are some vocabulary words you can use when you talk about light, sound, and electricity with your friends, family, and others.

acoustics—the science of sound. Acoustics is applied to the design of buildings. (**C68**)

aperture—an opening through which light comes into a camera. The size of the aperture is adjusted to let in different amounts of light. (**C36**)

▲ **Aperture**

color—a characteristic determined by the rays of light reflected by an object. Red objects reflect red light. White objects reflect nearly all light. (**C46**)

conductor—matter that allows electricity to flow through it. Wire and salt water are excellent conductors. (**C77**)

cones—cells in the retina of the eye that allow us to see color. (**C45**)

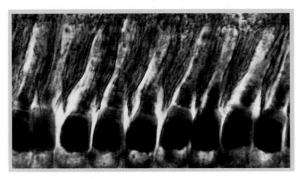

▲ **Cones and rods**

current—the flow of negatively charged atomic particles called *electrons*. In a *direct current* (DC) system, electrons travel in only one direction. In an *alternating current* (AC) system, electrons travel in a rotating wire coil placed in a magnetic field. As the coil rotates, the electrons continue to change direction. (**C74**)

electric circuit—a closed pathway for electricity to follow. In a series circuit, the current has only one path to follow. In a parallel circuit, the current has more than one path to follow. (**C72**)

insulator—a nonconductor of electric current. Glass and rubber are good insulators. (**C77**)

opaque—not allowing light rays to pass through. *Translucent* objects allow some light to pass through. *Transparent* objects allow all light to pass through. (**C22**)

persistence of vision—the holding of an image on the retina for a fraction of a second, making it possible for us to see a series of still images as motion. **(C33)**

pitch—the sound quality determined by the number of vibrations per second, measured in *hertz*. In music, different tones have different pitches. **(C64)**

primary colors of light—red, blue, and green, which can be combined to produce all other colors of the visible spectrum. **(C41)**

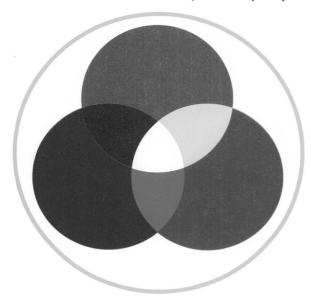

prism—a piece of glass with triangular bases that refracts white light into the visible spectrum: red, orange, yellow, green, blue, violet. **(C40)**

ray model—a way for scientists to show how rays of light travel. **(C20)**

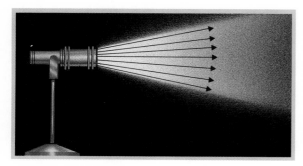

▲ **Ray model**

reflection—the bouncing of light rays. A smooth surface such as a mirror provides a clear reflected image that you can see. **(C23)**

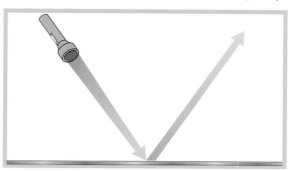

▲ **Reflection**

refraction—the bending of light rays. **(C28)**

◀ **Raindrops act as tiny prisms, refracting sunlight to form a rainbow.**

resistance—the property of matter that causes it to oppose the flow of electricity. The filament in a light bulb heats up and glows because of resistance. **(C74)**

rods—cells in the retina that help a person see in dim light. **(C45)**

volume—the loudness or softness of sounds. Volume is measured in decibels. Continued exposure to sounds of 100 decibels or more can damage the ears. **(C64)**

REFERENCE HANDBOOK

Safety in the Classroom

Doing activities in science can be fun, but you need to be sure you do them safely. It is up to you, your teacher, and your classmates to make your classroom a safe place for science activities.

Think about what causes most accidents in everyday life—being careless, not paying attention, and showing off. The same kinds of behavior cause accidents in the science classroom.

Here are some ways to make your classroom a safe place.

WATCH YOUR EYES.
Wear safety goggles anytime you are directed to do so. If you should ever get any substance in your eyes, tell your teacher right away.

THINK AHEAD.
Study the steps of the activity so you know what to expect. If you have any questions about the steps, ask your teacher to explain. Be sure you understand any safety symbols that are shown in the activity.

BE NEAT.
Keep your work area clean. If you have long hair, pull it back so it doesn't get in the way. If you have long sleeves, roll them or push them up to keep them away from your experiment.

YUCK!
Never eat or drink anything during a science activity unless you are told to do so by your teacher.

OOPS!
If you should have an accident that causes a spill or breaks something, or if you get cut, tell your teacher right away.

KEEP IT CLEAN.
Always clean up when you have finished your activity. Put everything away and wipe your work area. Last of all, wash your hands.

DON'T GET SHOCKED.
Sometimes you need to use electric appliances, such as lamps, in an activity. You always need to be careful around electricity. Be sure that electric cords are in a safe place where you can't trip over them. Don't ever pull a plug out of an outlet by pulling on the cord.

Safety Symbols

In some activities, you will see a symbol that stands for what you need to do to stay safe. Do what the symbol stands for.

 This is a general symbol that tells you to be careful. Reading the steps of the activity will tell you exactly what you need to do to be safe.

 You will need to protect your eyes if you see this symbol. Put on safety goggles and leave them on for the entire activity.

 This symbol tells you that you will be using something sharp in the activity. Be careful not to cut or poke yourself or others.

 This symbol tells you something hot will be used in the activity. Be careful not to get burned or to cause someone else to get burned.

 This symbol tells you to put on an apron to protect your clothing.

 Don't touch! This symbol tells you that you will need to touch something that is hot. Use a thermal mitt to protect your hand.

 This symbol tells you that you will be using electric equipment. Use proper safety procedures.

Using a Hand Lens

A hand lens magnifies objects, or makes them look larger than they are.

▲ This object is not in focus.

Sometimes objects are too small for you to see easily without some help. You might want to see details that you cannot see with your eyes alone. When this happens, you can use a hand lens.

To use a hand lens, first place the object you want to look at on a flat surface, such as a table. Next, hold the hand lens over the object. At first, the object may appear blurry, like the object in **A**. Move the hand lens toward or away from the object until the object comes into sharp focus, as shown in **B**.

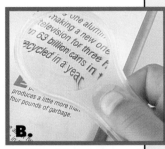

▲ This object is focused clearly.

Making a Water-Drop Lens

There may be times when you want to use a hand lens but there isn't one around. If that happens, you can make a water-drop lens to help you in the same way a hand lens does. A water-drop lens is best used to make flat objects, such as pieces of paper and leaves, seem larger.

MATERIALS
- sheet of acetate
- 2 rectangular rubber erasers
- water
- dropper

DO THIS

❶ Place the object to be magnified on a table between two identical erasers.

❷ Place a sheet of acetate on top of the erasers so that the sheet of acetate is about 1 cm above the object.

❸ Use the dropper to place one drop of water on the surface of the sheet over the object. Don't make the drop too large or it will make things look bent.

▶ A water-drop lens can magnify objects.

Caring For and Using a Microscope

A microscope, like a hand lens, magnifies objects. However, a microscope can increase the detail you see by increasing the number of times an object is magnified.

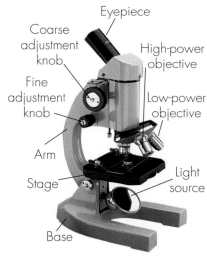

▲ **Light microscope**

CARING FOR A MICROSCOPE

* Always use two hands when you carry a microscope.
* Never touch any of the lenses of the microscope with your fingers.

USING A MICROSCOPE

❶ Raise the eyepiece as far as you can using the coarse-adjustment knob. Place the slide you wish to view on the stage.

❷ Always start by using the lowest power. The lowest-power lens is usually the shortest. Start with the lens in the lowest position it can go without touching the slide.

❸ Look through the eyepiece and begin adjusting the eyepiece upward with the coarse-adjustment knob. When the slide is close to being in focus, use the fine-adjustment knob.

❹ When you want to use the higher-power lens, first focus the slide under low power. Then, watching carefully to make sure that the lens will not hit the slide, turn the higher-power lens into place. Use only the fine-adjustment knob when looking through the higher-power lens.

Some of you may use a Brock microscope. This is a sturdy microscope that has only one lens.

❶ Place the object to be viewed on the stage. Move the long tube, containing the lens, close to the stage.

❷ Put your eye on the eyepiece, and begin raising the tube until the object comes into focus.

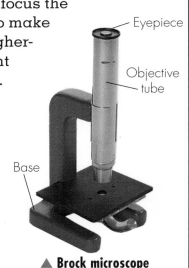

▲ **Brock microscope**

Using a Dropper

Use a dropper when you need to add small amounts of a liquid to another material.

A dropper has two main parts. One is a large empty part called a *bulb*. You hold the bulb and squeeze it to use the dropper. The other part of a dropper is long and narrow and is called a *tube*.

Droppers measure liquids one drop at a time. You might need to figure out how much liquid is in one drop. To do that, you can count the number of drops in 1 mL and divide. For example, if there are about 10 drops in 1 mL, you know that each drop is equal to about 0.1 mL. Follow the directions below to measure a liquid by using a dropper.

DO THIS

1 Use a clean dropper for each liquid you measure.

2 With the dropper out of the liquid, squeeze the bulb and keep it squeezed. Then dip the end of the tube into the liquid.

3 Release the pressure on the bulb. As you do so, you will see the liquid enter the tube.

4 Take the dropper from the liquid, and move it to the place you want to put the liquid. If you are putting the liquid into another liquid, do not let the dropper touch the surface of the second liquid.

5 Gently squeeze the bulb until one drop comes out of the tube. Repeat slowly until you have measured out the right number of drops.

▲ Using a dropper correctly

▲ Using a dropper incorrectly

Measuring Liquids

Use a beaker, a measuring cup, or a graduated cylinder to measure liquids accurately.

Containers for measuring liquids are made of clear or translucent materials so that you can see the liquid inside them. On the outside of each of these measuring tools, you will see lines and numbers that make up a scale. On most of the containers used by scientists, the scale is in milliliters (mL).

DO THIS

❶ Pour the liquid you want to measure into one of the measuring containers. Make sure your measuring container is on a flat, stable surface, with the measuring scale facing you.

❷ Look at the liquid through the container. Move so that your eyes are even with the surface of the liquid in the container.

❸ To read the volume of the liquid, find the scale line that is even with the top of the liquid. In narrow containers, the surface of the liquid may look curved. Take your reading at the lowest point of the curve.

❹ Sometimes the surface of the liquid may not be exactly even with a line. In that case, you will need to estimate the volume of the liquid. Decide which line the liquid is closer to, and use that number.

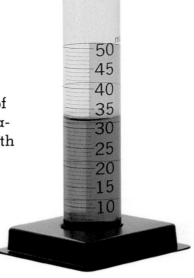

▲ There are 32 mL of liquid in this graduated cylinder.

▲ There are 27 mL of liquid in this beaker.

Using a Thermometer

Determine temperature readings of the air and most liquids by using a thermometer with a standard scale.

Most thermometers are thin tubes of glass that are filled with a red or silver liquid. As the temperature goes up, the liquid in the tube rises. As the temperature goes down, the liquid sinks. The tube is marked with lines and numbers that provide a temperature scale in degrees. Scientists use the Celsius scale to measure temperature. A temperature reading of 27 degrees Celsius is written 27°C.

DO THIS

❶ Place the thermometer in the liquid whose temperature you want to record, but don't rest the bulb of the thermometer on the bottom or side of the container. If you are measuring the temperature of the air, make sure that the thermometer is not in direct sunlight or in line with a direct light source.

❷ Move so that your eyes are even with the liquid in the thermometer.

❸ If you are measuring a material that is not being heated or cooled, wait about two minutes for the reading to become stable. Find the scale line that meets the top of the liquid in the thermometer, and read the temperature.

❹ If the material you are measuring is being heated or cooled, you will not be able to wait before taking your measurements. Measure as quickly as you can.

▶ The temperature of this liquid is 27°C.

Making a Thermometer

If you don't have a thermometer, you can make a simple one easily. The simple thermometer won't give you an exact temperature reading, but you can use it to tell if the temperature is going up or going down.

DO THIS

1 Add colored water to the jar until it is nearly full.

2 Place the straw in the jar. Finish filling the jar with water, but leave about 1 cm of space at the top.

3 Lift the straw until 10 cm of it stick up out of the jar. Use the clay to seal the mouth of the jar.

4 Use the dropper to add colored water to the straw until the straw is at least half full.

5 On the straw, mark the level of the water. "S" stands for *start*.

6 To get an idea of how your thermometer works, place the jar in a bowl of ice. Wait several minutes, and then mark the new water level on the straw. This new water level should be marked C for *cold*.

7 Take the jar out of the bowl of ice, and let it return to room temperature. Next, place the jar in a bowl of warm water. Wait several minutes, and then mark the new water level on the straw. This level can be labeled W for *warm*.

▶ You can use a thermometer like this to decide if the temperature of a liquid or the air is going up or down.

Using a Balance

Use a balance to measure an object's mass. Mass is the amount of matter an object has.

Most balances look like the one shown. They have two pans. In one pan, you place the object you want to measure. In the other pan, you place standard masses. Standard masses are objects that have a known mass. Grams are the units used to measure mass for most scientific activities.

DO THIS

❶ First, make certain the empty pans are balanced. They are in balance if the pointer is at the middle mark on the base. If the pointer is not at this mark, move the slider to the right or left. Your teacher will help if you cannot balance the pans.

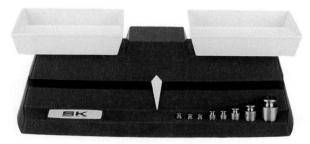

◀ **These pans are balanced and ready to be used to find the mass of an object.**

❷ Place the object you wish to measure in one pan. The pointer will move toward the pan without the object in it.

❸ Add the standard masses to the other pan. As you add masses, you should see the pointer begin to move. When the pointer is at the middle mark again, the pans are balanced.

❹ Add the numbers on the masses you used. The total is the mass of the object you measured.

▶ **These pans are unbalanced.**

Making a Balance

If you do not have a balance, you can make one. A balance requires only a few simple materials. You can use nonstandard masses such as paper clips or nickels. This type of balance is best for measuring small masses.

DO THIS

1 If the ruler has holes in it, tie the string through the center hole. If it does not have holes, tie the string around the middle of the ruler.

2 Tape the other end of the string to a table. Allow the ruler to hang down from the side of the table. Adjust the ruler so that it is level.

3 Unbend the end of each paper clip slightly. Push these ends through the paper cups as shown. Attach each cup to the ruler by using the paper clips.

4 Adjust the cups until the ruler is level again.

MATERIALS
- 1 sturdy plastic or wooden ruler
- string
- transparent tape
- 2 paper cups
- 2 large paper clips

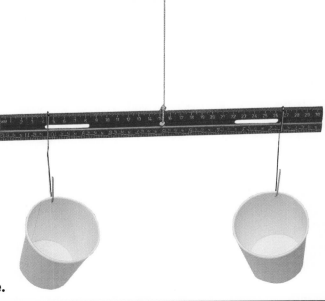

▶ **This balance is ready for use.**

Using a Spring Scale

A spring scale is a tool you use to measure the force of gravity on objects. You find the weight of the objects and use newtons as the unit of measurement for the force of gravity. You also use the spring scale and newtons to measure other forces.

A spring scale has two main parts. One part is a spring with a hook on the end. The hook is used to connect an object to the spring scale. The other part is a scale with numbers that tell you how many newtons of force are acting on the object.

DO THIS

With an Object at Rest

1 With the object resting on the table, hook the spring scale to it. Do not stretch the spring at this point.

2 Lift the scale and object with a smooth motion. Do not jerk them upward.

3 Wait until any motion in the spring comes to a stop. Then read the number of newtons from the scale.

With an Object in Motion

1 With the object resting on the table, hook the spring scale to it. Do not stretch the spring.

2 Pull the object smoothly across the table. Do not jerk the object. If you pull with a jerky motion, the spring scale will wiggle too much for you to get a good reading.

3 As you are pulling, read the number of newtons you are using to pull the object.

Making a Spring Scale

If you do not have a spring scale, you can make one by following the directions below.

DO THIS

1 Staple one end of the rubber band (the part with the sharp curve) to the middle of one end of the cardboard so that the rubber band hangs down the length of the cardboard. Color the loose end of the rubber band with a marker to make it easy to see.

2 Bend the paper clip so that it is slightly open and forms a hook. Hang the paper clip by its unopened end from the rubber band.

3 Put the narrow paper strip across the rubber band, and staple the strip to the cardboard. The rubber band and hook must be able to move easily.

4 While holding the cardboard upright, hang one 100-g mass from the hook. Allow the mass to come to rest, and mark the position of the bottom of the rubber band on the cardboard. Label this position on the cardboard 1 N. Add another 100-g mass for a total of 200 g.

5 Continue to add masses and mark the cardboard. Each 100-g mass adds a force of about 1 N.

MATERIALS

- heavy cardboard (10cm x 30cm)
- large rubber band
- stapler
- marker
- large paper clip
- paper strip (about 1 cm x 3 cm)
- 100-g masses (about 1 N each)

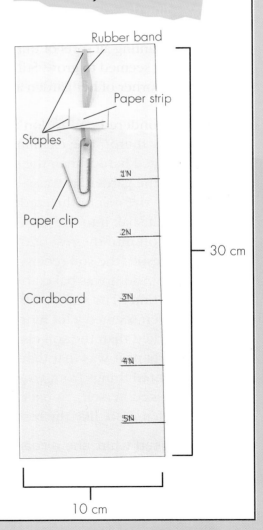

Rubber band

Paper strip

Staples

Paper clip

Cardboard

1 N

2 N

3 N

4 N

5 N

30 cm

10 cm

After you have suggested an answer to your question, you must develop a way to test that answer. Sometimes you may choose to build a model to answer your question. Building models was one way questions were answered in the early years of building aircraft. Sometimes you can't make a model and you can't really do an experiment. Then you might choose to record detailed observations of natural occurrences to find an answer. For instance, if you wanted to know the types of fossils in different layers of rocks, you would collect the rocks and make detailed observations. But the approach to solving problems in science that most people are aware of is experimenting. An *experiment* is a planned test under controlled conditions. An experiment should test the solution you have proposed. The experiment should be repeatable by other people who study similar things.

An experiment must be carefully planned. You change only one variable at a time. Suppose Alexia wanted to test the effect of watering the soil more. She might add different amounts of water to different samples of soil. But the samples should otherwise be as nearly the same as possible—for example, in the materials they contain.

DO THIS

| Ask a question. |
| Form a hypothesis. |
| Design a test. Do the test. |
| Record what happened. |
| Draw a conclusion. |

In addition, an experiment often includes a control. A *control* is a sample that you do not treat in any unusual way. The control serves as a standard for comparison. For example, if Alexia chose to test the effects of different amounts of water, her control would be a soil sample receiving the amount of water that is usual for her garden. Then, if Alexia discovered that plants grew just as well in the control as in the other samples, she would know that watering was not an important factor.

Adding something to loosen the soil is the answer that Alexia chose for her hypothesis. She wanted to develop a way to test it.

She went into the garage and looked at her gardening supplies. She had potting soil, some sand, some fertilizer, and some vermiculite, a material that has highly water-absorbent particles in it. At one time or another, she had added all of these things to the soil of her garden. Maybe some of these things would make the soil looser. How could she find out?

Alexia knew that water flowed through looser soil more swiftly. She could test her soils by seeing how long it took for water to flow through them.

After she had gotten her parents' permission, she designed her experiment. She needed to dry out five equal-sized samples of the soil from the part of the gar-den where nothing grew. She would do nothing to one of the sam-ples. To each of the other samples, she would add one of the things she had found in the garage.

When she had done that, she found some wide plastic tubes. She placed each of her soils into a different plastic tube. She made sure that all of the tubes had the same amount of soil. She added the same amount of water to each tube and recorded the amount of time it took for the water to seep through the soil.

Data is another word for information. The data from an experiment includes observations and measurements. It is important that everything about an experiment is carefully recorded—not only the data but also the problem you are investigating, the methods you use, and the solution you propose. Other people who work on the same problem should be able to do your experiment again and see if they come up with the same or similar results.

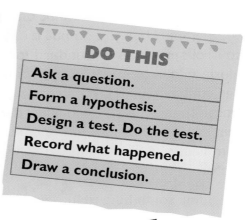

DO THIS

Ask a question.
Form a hypothesis.
Design a test. Do the test.
Record what happened.
Draw a conclusion.

Scientists use many different ways to *record data.* Two of the most common ways are making tables and making graphs. These are very useful because they help to organize the information that is collected. They serve as a summary of the results of an experiment. Think about it—if you had to write out each of your measurements and observations in a separate sentence, the report on the experiment would be very long. However, you can shorten all of that by recording the data in a table. Sometimes, depending on the data, you can make a graph to serve as a visual summary. Looking at the data in more than one way can make some of the results clearer.

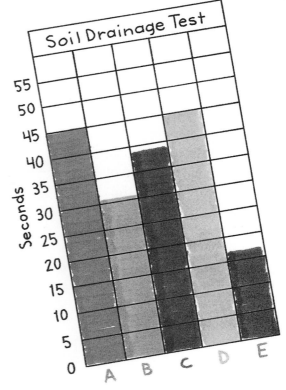

Soil Drainage Test

	Soil Drainage Test Results	
	Material	Time
A	Plain Soil	45 Seconds
B	Soil/Sand	31 Seconds
C	Soil/Potting Soil	38 Seconds
D	Soil/Fertilizer	45 Seconds
E	Soil/Vermiculite	17 Seconds

Alexia made a table to record the time it took the water to reach the bottom of each tube. The table summarized her information, but Alexia thought that she should look at the data in another way. The table and graph summarize what Alexia discovered. Through which soil did water run most rapidly?

DO THIS

| Ask a question. |
| Form a hypothesis. |
| Design a test. Do the test. |
| Record what happened. |
| Draw a conclusion. |

There is no point at all to doing an experiment if you do not reach some sort of conclusion. You might conclude that your hypothesis was incorrect. You might conclude that the experiment did not give enough information and that another test must be performed.

You *draw a conclusion* when you analyze the data and decide whether your hypothesis is supported or not. You use what you already know about the situation to decide what your data is telling you.

Alexia saw that the soil with the vermiculite allowed water to run through it the fastest. She concluded that if she used vermiculite in the corner of her garden, the soil might be loose enough for water to soak through more easily and, therefore, plants might grow there.

You can see that Alexia reached a conclusion. Part of her hypothesis was supported. However, another part of her hypothesis was not tested. Remember, she thought that making the soil looser would enable plants to grow. Alexia did not test plant growth. So she had support for one part of her hypothesis, but she must design another experiment to test the other part.

INDEX

D

Insulator
  activity, C76–C77
  defined, C77, C94
Internet, A7, B7, D7, F7
Interpreting data, A10
Invertebrates, D40–*D41*
  defined, D40
Iran, earthquake in, A61
Iris (eye), *C30*, C31
Iris (flower), *B31*
Italy, as land of volcanoes, A64–A66
Ivory, *B83*
"I Wandered Lonely as a Cloud"
  (Wordsworth), F52
Izaak Walton League of America, F7

Jackson, Marjorie, C17–C18
Jacobs, Linda, E9
Jaguar, *B3*, *B85*
Japan, myth from, A51
Jason Junior (JJ), D69, D80, *D81*, D84
JASON Project, D85, *D86–D87*
Jellyfish, D51, *D53*
Jet airplanes, sound of, *C65*
JIM suit, *D25*, D88, *D89*
Journey Through a Tropical Jungle
  (Forsyth), B9
June 29, 1999 (Wiesner), F9
"Jungle Journey, A" (*Ranger Rick's
  NatureScope®*), B33–B35
Jupiter, *A15*
Just a Dream (Van Allsburg), E8

Kaleidoscope, activity, *C42*
Kangaroo legend, B64–B65
Kashima, A51
Kavieng Island, Papua, New Guinea,
  D14–D15
Kerosene, E65, E66
Key
  activity, B16
  defined, B16, B95
  for trees, *B17*
Key deer, *B77*, *B88*
Kilauea (volcano), *A69*, A70
Kinetic energy
  activity, E20
  defined, E19, E111
Kingdom(s), defined, B14, B95
Kiwi(s), *B76*, *F35*
Knees (bald cypress tree), F84
Kooyman, Dr. Shirley, F88–*F89*
Kramer, Alan, A9
Krohn, Daniel, D37
Kuwait, oil fire in, *E83*, E84

Lake Ontario, D87

Language of science
  abyss, D54, D94
  acid rain, E75, E110
  acoustics, C68, C94
  adaptation, B62, *B94*
  angiosperms, F38, F94
  animal, B14, B94
  anticlines, A41, A78
  aperture, C36, *C94*
  atoll, D20, D94
  bioluminescence, D52, D94
  biomass, E41, E110
  botanist, B14, B94
  buoyancy, D22, *D94*
  chemical energy, E16, E110
  chlorophyll, F21, F94
  chloroplast, F21, F94
  circuit, C72, C94
  classifying, B14, B94
  color, C46, C94
  compression, A41, A78
  conductor, C77, C94, E55, E110
  cones, C45, *C94*
  continental drift, A22, A78
  core, *A18*, A78
  cotyledons, F55, F94
  crust, *A18*, A78
  current electricity, C74, C94, E17,
    E110
  currents, D64, D94
  ecotone, D38, D94
  electric energy, E17, *E110*, E111
  electrons, C74, C94
  embryo, F55, F94
  endangered, B78, B94
  energy, E13, E111
  epidermis, F18, F94
  estuary, D44, D94
  evolution, B69, B94
  extinct, B68, B94
  fault, A42, A78
  fertilization, F47, F94
  folding, A41, *A79*
  fracture, A42, A79
  fungus, B24, *B95*
  gasification, E59, E111
  gasohol, E68, E111
  generator, E29, E111
  geothermal energy, E39, *E111*
  germinate, F55, F94
  gymnosperms, F38, *F94*
  habitat, B78, B95
  heterozygous, F64, F94
  homozygous, F64, F94
  hydrocarbons, E33, E111
  hydroelectric energy, E51, E111
  insulator, C77, C94
  key, B16, B95
  kilowatt-hour, E94, E111
  kinetic energy, E19, E111
  kingdom, B14, B95
  lava, A69, A79
  magnitude, A60, A79
  mantle, *A18*, A79
  mechanical energy, E13, E111
  meristem, F34, F94
  moneran, B24, *B95*
  natural selection, B62, B95
  nonrenewable resources, E89, E111
  nonvascular plants, F38, F94
  nuclear energy, E18, E111
  opaque, C22, C94
  Pangea, *A21*, A79
  persistence of vision, C33, C95

  petals, F46, F94
  petroleum, E63, E111
  phloem, F29, F95
  photosynthesis, F21, F95
  photosynthetic zone, D50, D95
  pitch, C64, C95
  plant, B14, B95
  plate tectonics, A27, A79
  pollination, F47, F95
  potential energy, E19, *E111*
  primary colors of light, C41, *C95*
  prism, C40, C95
  protist, B24, *B95*
  radiant energy, E15, *E111*
  ray model, C20, *C95*
  reflection, C26, *C95*
  refraction, C28, *C95*
  remote sensors, D29, D95
  renewable resources, E89, E112
  resistance, C74, C95
  Richter scale, A60, A79
  Ring of Fire, A30–A31, A79
  rods, C45, C95
  root, F34, *F95*
  scuba, D25, D95
  seed coat, F55, *F95*
  seedless vascular plants, F41, F95
  seismograph, *A19*, *A79*
  sepals, F46, F95
  shear, A44, A79
  smog, E86, E112
  snorkel, D24, D95
  solar energy, E53, E112
  sonar, D28, *D29*, D95
  species, B15, B95
  stem, F28, F95
  stimulus, F70, F95
  stomata, F18, F95
  submersibles, D26, D95
  synclines, A41, A79
  synthetic fuel, E60, E112
  tension, A44, A79
  thermal energy, E14, *D112*
  threatened, B78, B95
  tide(s), D58, *D95*
  tide pool, D40, *D95*
  traits, F63, F95
  transformer, E29, E112
  tropism, F70, *F95*
  turbine, E29, E112
  vascular plants, F38, *F95*
  vegetative reproduction, F59, F95
  voltage, E54, E112
  volume, C64, C95
  walls, A42, A79
  water cycle, D48, *D95*
  waves, A54, *A79*
  wind turbine, E50, E112
  xylem, F29, F95
Lasky, Kathryn, A9
Lateral fault, *A44*
Latex, *B50*
Latimer, Lewis Howard, C7
Lava, *A69*
  activity, A68
  defined, A69, A79
Lawren, Bill, C78–C79
Laws, environmental protection, B79,
  B81
Leaf–cutter ants, *B34*
Leaf–shaped moth, B34
Leaves, F13–F25, *F17*, *F18*
  activities, F14, F15, F16, F19
  architecture of, F17–F18

ACKNOWLEDGMENTS

For permission to reprint copyrighted material, grateful acknowledgment is made to the following sources:

Harry N. Abrams, Inc.: Cover illustration from *The Sign of the Seahorse* by Graeme Base. Copyright © 1992 by Doublebase Pty. Ltd.

Boys' Life Magazine: From "'The Titanic Has Gone Down!'" and from "They've Found the Titanic" (Retitled: "Finding the Titanic" and "They Found the Titanic") by Jon C. Halter in *Boys' Life* Magazine. Text © 1989 by the Boy Scouts of America. Reprinted from the October and November 1989 issues. Published by Boy Scouts of America.

Children's Better Health Institute, Indianapolis, IN: "Desert Plants: Secrets of Survival" by Eileen Ross from *Children's Playmate* Magazine, January/February 1993. Text copyright © 1992 by Children's Better Health Institute, Benjamin Franklin Literary & Medical Society, Inc.

Clarion Books, a Houghton Mifflin Company imprint: Cover illustration from *Cartons, Cans, and Orange Peels: Where Does Your Garbage Go?* by Joanna Foster. Copyright © 1991 by Joanna Foster.

Cobblestone Publishing, Inc., 7 School Street, Peterborough, NH 03458: "Gusher!" by Roberta Baxter, "From Muscle Power to Atomic Power" by Karen E. Hong, and "The War of the Currents" by Richard L. Mattis from *Cobblestone: Energy, Powering Our Nation*, October 1990. Text © 1990 by Cobblestone Publishing, Inc. From "Philo Farnsworth: Forgotten Inventor" by Jeanne Field Olson in *Cobblestone: Tuning In to Television*, October 1989. Text © 1989 by Cobblestone Publishing, Inc. "The Daguerreotype in America" by June L. Sargent from *Cobblestone: The Art of Photography*, April 1985. Text © 1985 by Cobblestone Publishing, Inc.

Dial Books for Young Readers, a division of Penguin Books USA Inc.: Cover illustration from *A Flower Grows* by Ken Robbins. Copyright © 1990 by Ken Robbins.

Disney Magazine Publishing, Inc.: "Deep Trouble" from *Disney Adventures: The Magazine for Kids*, September 1993. © by Disney.

Harcourt Brace & Company: Cover photograph by Michael Wallace from *On the Brink of Extinction: The California Condor* by Caroline Arnold. Photograph copyright © 1993 by Greater Los Angeles Zoo Association Condor Fund. Cover illustration by Tatsuro Kiuchi from *The Lotus Seed* by Sherry Garland. Illustration copyright © 1993 by Tatsuro Kiuchi. Cover illustration by David Kahl from *Earthquake at Dawn* by Kristiana Gregory. Copyright © 1992 by Kristiana Gregory.

HarperCollins Publishers: From *The Clover & the Bee: A Book of Pollination* by Anne Ophelia Dowden. Text copyright © 1990 by Anne Ophelia Dowden. Cover illustration by Dan Brown from *The Missing 'Gator of Gumbo Limbo: An Ecological Mystery* by Jean Craighead George. Illustration © 1992 by Dan Brown.

Henry Holt and Company, Inc.: "Gathering Leaves" by Robert Frost from *The Poetry of Robert Frost*, edited by Edward Connery Lathem. Text copyright 1951 by Robert Frost; text copyright 1923, © 1969 by Henry Holt and Company, Inc.

Holt, Rinehart and Winston, Inc.: "Karen McNally, Seismologist" from *Holt Earth Science* by Robert Fronk and Linda Knight. Text copyright © 1994 by Holt, Rinehart and Winston, Inc.

Houghton Mifflin Company: Cover illustration from *Just a Dream* by Chris Van Allsburg. Copyright © 1990 by Chris Van Allsburg.

Houston Chronicle: From "Field Days in the Marsh" by Kevin Moran in *Houston Chronicle*, July 18, 1993. Text © by Houston Chronicle.

Hyperion Books for Children, an imprint of Disney Book Publishing Group, Inc.: Cover photograph by Sigurgeir Jónasson from *Surtsey: The Newest Place on Earth* by Kathryn Lasky, photographs by Christopher G. Knight. Cover photograph copyright © 1992 by Sigurgeir Jónasson.

Marjorie Jackson: "Shadow Puppets of Indonesia" by Marjorie Jackson from *Cricket* Magazine, January 1992. Text © 1992 by Marjorie Jackson.

Alfred A. Knopf, Inc.: Cover illustration by David J. Catrow from *Backstage with Clawdio* by Harriet Berg Schwartz. Illustration copyright © 1993 by David J. Catrow.

Lodestar Books, an affiliate of Dutton Children's Books, a division of Penguin Books USA Inc.: From *Amy: The Story of a Deaf Child* by Lou Ann Walker, photographs by Michael Abramson. Text copyright © 1985 by Lou Ann Walker; photographs copyright © 1985 by Michael Abramson.

Macmillan Publishing Company, a Division of Macmillan, Inc.: "How Gray the Rain" from *Five Bushel Farm* by Elizabeth Coatsworth. Text copyright 1939 by Macmillan Publishing Company, renewed 1967 by Elizabeth Coatsworth Beston. "Why Most Trees and Plants Have Flat Leaves" from *Hidden Stories in Plants* by Anne Pellowski. Text copyright © 1990 by Anne Pellowski.

Morrow Junior Books, a division of William Morrow & Company, Inc.: Cover photograph by Richard Hewett from *Look Alive: Behind the Scenes of an Animated Film* by Elaine Scott. Photograph © 1992 by Richard Hewett. From pp. 54–55 in *RAMONA: Behind the Scenes of a Television Show* by Elaine Scott, photograph by Margaret Miller. Text copyright © 1988 by Elaine Scott; photograph copyright © 1988 by Margaret Miller.

National Geographic Books for World Explorers: From pp. 43–44 in *Dolphins: Our Friends in the Sea* by Judith E. Rinard. Text copyright 1986 by National Geographic Society.

National Geographic Society: From "A Walk in the Deep" by Sylvia A. Earle in *National Geographic* Magazine, May 1980. Text copyright © 1980 by National Geographic Society.

National Geographic WORLD: "Driven by Cars" from *National Geographic WORLD* Magazine, May 1991. Text copyright 1991 by National Geographic Society. "Meet...Bob Ballard, Undersea Explorer" from *National Geographic WORLD* Magazine, December 1993. Text copyright 1993 by National Geographic Society. Illustration by Dale Glasgow. "Hot! Conquering Oil Fires" by Ross Bankson from *National Geographic WORLD* Magazine, May 1992. Text copyright 1992 by National Geographic Society.

National Wildlife Federation: "RAP Team to the Rescue" by Deborah Churchman from *Ranger Rick* Magazine, April 1993. Text copyright 1993 by the National Wildlife Federation. "The Puzzling Platypus" by Kathy Walsh from *Ranger Rick* Magazine, May 1992. Text copyright 1992 by the National Wildlife Federation. "Away on the Bay" from *Ranger Rick's NatureScope®, Pollution: Problems and Solutions*. Copyright 1990 by the National Wildlife Federation. From "A Jungle Journey" in *Ranger Rick's NatureScope®, Rain Forests: Tropical Treasures*. Copyright 1989 by the National Wildlife Federation.

OMNI Publications International, Ltd.: Adapted from "Rediscovering Tesla" by Bill Lawren in *OMNI* Magazine, March 1988. Text © 1988 by OMNI Publications International, Ltd.

Jane R. Ray: "Shadow Puppets" cover illustration by Jane R. Ray from *Cricket* Magazine, January 1992.

Kay Saetre: From "Living by a Volcano" by Kay Saetre in *Cricket* Magazine, June 1985. Text © 1985 by Kay Saetre.

Thames and Hudson Inc.: Cover photograph by Len Rubenstein from *Real Kids Real Science, Marine Biology* by Ellen Doris. Copyright © 1993 by Thames and Hudson.

Viking Penguin, a division of Penguin Books USA Inc.: "How the People Sang the Mountains Up" from *How the People Sang the Mountains Up* by Maria Leach. Text copyright © 1967 by Maria Leach.

Franklin Watts Inc., New York: From *The Voyage of the Beagle* by Kate Hyndley. Text copyright © 1989 by Wayland (Publishers) Limited.

PHOTOGRAPHY CREDITS:
Key: (t)top, (b)bottom, (l)left, (r)right, (c)center, (bg)background

Front Cover, Harcourt Brace & Company Photographs: (bl), (br), Greg Leary.
Front Cover, All Other Photographs: (t) Fujiphotos/The Image Works; (cl), Tom Walker AllStock; (c), Paul Chesley /Tony Stone Images.
Back Cover, Harcourt Brace & Company Photographs: (t), (bl), Greg Leary.
Front Cover, All Other Photographs: (br) Porterfield Chickering/Photo Researchers.
To The Student, Harcourt Brace & Company Photographs: iv(bc), Greg Leary; v(bl), Weronica Ankarorn; vi(tl), Photo Studio; viii(bc), David Phillips; xi(t), Delinda Karnehm; xiv(r), Terry McManamy.
To The Student, All Other Photographs: iv(t), The Granger Collection; iv(bl), Photri/ The Stock Market; iv(br), Pictor/Uniphoto; v(t), Stephen Dalton/Photo Researchers; v(br), Brian Parker/Tom Stack & Assoc.; vi(tr), Richard Adams; vi(c), Grag Vaughn/ Tom Stack & Assoc.; vi(bl), SuperStock; vi(br), H.R. Bramaz/Peter Arnold, Inc.; vii(tl), Mike Bacon/Tom Stack & Assoc.; vii(b-inset), Kjell Sandved/Uniphoto; viii(tl), Damm/ Zefa/H. Armstrong Roberts, Inc.; viii(tr), Keith Kent/Peter Arnold, Inc.; viii(br), The Bettmann Archive; ix(tl), H. Armstrong Roberts, Inc.; ix(tr) SuperStock; ix(tc), Uniphoto; ix(bc), Scott Camazine/Photo Researchers; ix(b), SuperStock; x, David Young-Wolff/PhotoEdit; xi(b) Michael S. Thompson/Comstock; xii, Gabe Palmer/The Stock Market; xiii, Bruce M. Wellman/Stock, Boston; xiv(l) Comstock; xv(t), Mary Kate Denny/PhotoEdit; xv(b), Superstock; xvi(l), David Young-Wolff/PhotoEdit; xvi(r), Amy C. Etra/PhotoEdit.
Unit A, Harcourt Brace & Company Photographs: A4-A5, A6(t), A6(c), A6(b), A7, Greg Leary; A8, A9, Photo Studio; A10-A11, A12, A12(inset), A13, A16, A17, A18, A20, A23, A24, A25, A32, A33, A35, A40, A43, A46, A47, A52, A53, A55, A58, A68, A74-A75, A75(tc), A76(t), A76(b), A77(t), A77(b), Greg Leary.
Unit A, All Other Photographs: A01, Ric Ergenbright; Unit Divider Page, Salmioraghi/The Stock Market; A2-A3, Ric Ergenbright Photography; A3(inset), B.Barbey/Magnum Photos; A19, Reuters/Bettmann; A22, The Granger Collection, New York; A28, G.R. Roberts/ Documentary Photographs; A28, Richard Hutchings/Photo Researchers; A28(inset), Simon Fraser/Science Photo Library/Photo Researchers; A29(tr), Bob Abraham/The Stock Market; A29(br), A.Taylor/PhotoReporters; A29(l), Photri Inc./The Stock Market; A32-A33(bg), Paul Berger/Tony Stone Images; A34, Tony Waltham/Robert Harding Picture Library; A41, G.R.Roberts/Documentary Photographs; A42, Tony Stone Images; A44-A45(t), David R.Frazier; A44(b), Rick Browne/PhotoReporters; A45, A48-49(b), Ric Ergenbright Photography; A49, Bob Clemenz Photography; A50(bg), Robert Yager/Tony Stone Images; A50, Piotr Kapa/The Stock Market; A50(inset), Herman Kokojan/Black Star; A51, Lance Schriner-Holt, Rinehart & Winston; A56-57(t), Barbara Laing/Black Star; A56-57(b), Dennis Cipnic/Black Star; A57(inset), The Granger Collection, New York; A58-59(bg), E.Sander/Liaison International; A59(l), Tom Myers; A59(r), William S. Helsel/Tony Stone Images; A60(l), A60(r), E.Sander/Liaison International; A61(l), Noel Quidu/ Liaison International; A61(c), David Ryan/Uniphoto; A61(r), Pictor/Uniphoto; A62, A63, Don Fukuda/USC Photo Library; A64, Giraudon/Art Resource; A65(t), Scala/Art Resource; A65(bl), Mike Mazzaschi/Stock, Boston; A65(br), Figaro Magazine/Liaison International; A67, Ken Sakamoto/Black Star; A69(t), Franco Salmoiraghi/The Stock Market; A69(b), Rene Burri/Magnum; A74-A75(bg), Tony Stone Images; A75(tl), Photri Inc./The Stock Market; A75(tr), David Weintraub/Photo Researchers; A76-A77(bg), James Balog/Black Star; A79(l), G.R. Roberts/Documentary Photographs; A79(r), Tom Myers.
Unit B, Harcourt Brace & Company Photographs: B4-B5, Greg Leary; B8, B9, Photo Studio; B10-B11, B16, B22, B31(bl), B31(bc), B31(br), Greg Leary; B36-B37, B36(tl), Michael Smith/Black Star; B40, Rob Downey; B45, Greg Leary; B51, Weronica Ankarorn; B61, B70, B75, B80, B81, B82, B89, Greg Leary; B90-B91, Weronica Ankarorn; B91(tr), B92(t), Greg Leary; B92(b), Weronica Ankarorn; B93(t), Greg Leary.
Unit B, All Other Photographs: B01, Superstock; Unit Divider Page, Pat Crowe/Animals, Animals; B2-B3, SuperStock; B3, Alan D. Carey/Photo Researchers; B4-B5(bg), Julie Habel/ WestLight; B6(tr), SuperStock; B6(l), Tom & Pat Leeson/Photo Researchers; B6(br), Brian Parker/Tom Stack & Assoc.; B7, Roger Aitkenhead/Animals, Animals; B10-B11(bg), W. Cody/WestLight; B12(border), Aaron Haupt/David R. Frazier Photolibrary; B12(c),

Scenes; D74-D75, Drawing by Richard Schlecht/ National Geographic Society; D75(t), Bruce Dale/National Geographic Society; D75(b), Culver Pictures, Inc.; D76, APA/Archive Photos; D79, D80, Emory Kristof/National Geographic Society; D82(l), Emmett W. Francois; D82(r), Emory Kristof/National Geographic Society; D83, Dudley Foster/ Woods Hole Oceanographic Institute; D84(tl), Culver Pictures, Inc.; D84(c), Woods Hole Oceanographic Institute; D84(b), APA/Archive Photos; D85, SuperStock; D86(t), Artwork by Dale Glasgow/National Geographic Society; D86(b), Maria Stenzel/National Geographic Society; D87(t), Joseph H. Bailey/National Geographic Society; D87(c), © Quest Group, Ltd./The JASON Foundation/Woods Hole Oceanographic Institution; D87(b), Artwork by E. Paul Oberlander/Woods Hole Oceanographic Institution; D88, Charles Nicklin/Images Unlimited; D89(t), D89(b), Al Giddings/Images Unlimited; D90-D91(bg), Greg Vaughn/Tom Stack & Assoc.; D91(l), Christopher Swann/Peter Arnold, Inc.; D92-D93(bg), Emory Kristof/National Geographic Society; D93(t), Craig Newbauer/Peter Arnold, Inc.; D94, C.C. Lockwood/Animals, Animals; D95(tl), D95(tr), Stephen J. Krasemann/Peter Arnold, Inc.; D95(b), Larry Lefever/Grant Heilman Photography

Unit E. Harcourt Brace & Company Photographs: E4-E5, Greg Leary; E6(t), David Phillips; E6(b), Rich Franco; E8, E9, Photo Studio; E10-E11, Greg Leary; E13(t), E13(b), E14(b), Richard Nowitz; E15(t), E15(c), Weronica Ankarorn; E16(b), Richard Nowitz; E17(inset), Greg Leary; E21(inset), Maria Paraskavas; E22(t), E22(b-inset), E22-E23(t), E23(tr), E23(bl), David Phillips; E24, E32, E40, Richard Nowitz; E42, Maria Paraskavas; E44, Richard Nowitz; E45, David Phillips; E46, Weronica Ankarorn; E50(b), Maria Paraskavas; E56, E56(bg), Greg Leary; E61, E70, Maria Paraskavas; E75, E82, Richard Nowitz; E86, Weronica Ankarorn; E95, Rich Franco; E96, Richard Nowitz; E98(tr), E99(inset), Greg Leary; E106-E107, Photo Studio; E107(tc), E108(t), Rich Franco; E108-E109(b), Photo Studio; E109(t), E109(b), David Phillips; E110(t), Photo Studio.

Unit E. All Other Photographs: Unit Divider Page, IFA/Peter Arnold; E2-3(bg), Peter Arnold, Inc.; E3, E7(t), Comstock; E7(c), Kevin O. Mooney/photo taken at The Power House, Commonwealth Edison; E7(b), W. Perry Conway/Tom Stack & Assoc.; E12(c), Ray Pfortner/Peter Arnold, Inc.; E12(inset), L. Fritz/H. Armstrong Roberts, Inc.; E14(t), Malcolm Kirk/Peter Arnold, Inc.; E16(t), J. Patton/H. Armstrong Roberts, Inc.; E17(bg), Keith Kent/ Peter Arnold Inc.; E18, Douglas Faulkner/Photo Researchers; E19, Bruce Curtis/Peter Arnold, Inc.; E22(br), Alfred Pasieka/Peter Arnold, Inc.; E23(br), Tim Davis/Photo Researchers; E25(t), Spencer Grant/ Photo Researchers; E25(b), J. Gerard Smith/Photo Researchers; E26(border), W. Cody/ West-Light; E26(c), Jim Corwin/Photo Researchers; E26(inset), Matt Meadows/Peter Arnold, Inc.; E27(tl), Rafael Macia/Photo Researchers; E27(tc), H. Armstrong Roberts, Inc.; E27(tr), Photo Researchers; E27(bl), Alain Evrard/Photo Researchers; E27(bc), Lawrence Migdale/Photo Researchers; E27(br), Jack Elness/Comstock; E30, Jeri Gleiter/Peter Arnold, Inc.; E31, Earl Roberge/Photo Researchers; E33, Kage/Peter Arnold, Inc.; E34(l), Lowell Georgia Arctic Resources/Photo Researchers; E34(r), Harvey Lloyd/Peter Arnold, Inc.; E35(bg), E35, E36(t), Spindletop/Gladys City Boomtown Museum; E36(b), Drake Well Museum; E37, Spindletop/ Gladys City Boomtown Museum; E38(l), Australian Picture Library/WestLight; E38(r), U.S. Department of Energy; E39(t), W. Perry Conway/Tom Stack & Assoc.; E39(b), Randall Hyman; E41(t), Horst Schafer/Peter Arnold, Inc.; E41(c), Larry Lefever/Grant Heilman Photography; E41(b), Phil Degginger/Color-Pic, Inc.; E43, E.R. Degginger/Color-Pic, Inc.; E44-E45(bg), Tony Freeman/PhotoEdit; E47, E.R. Degginger/Color-Pic, Inc.; E48, E48-E49, Westinghouse Electric Corporation; E50(t), H.R. Bramaz/Peter Arnold, Inc.; E51, Brian Parker/Tom Stack & Assoc.; E52(tr), Martin Bond/Photo Researchers; E52(cl), Steven E. Sutton/Duomo Photography; E52(bl), Steven E. Sutton/Duomo Photography; E52(bc), Steven E. Sutton/Duomo Photography; E52-E53, Greg Vaughn/Tom Stack & Assoc.; E53(t), NASA; E53(b), Dingo/ Photo Researchers; E54(t), IFA/Peter Arnold, Inc.; E54(b), David R. Frazier Photo-library; E54-E55(bg), Thomas Kitchin/Tom Stack & Assoc.; E58(border), B. Kliewe/H. Armstrong Roberts, Inc.; E58(c), Bjorn Bolstad/Peter Arnold, Inc.; E58(inset), Damm/ Zefa/H. Armstrong Roberts, Inc.; E59(t), R. Michael Stuckey/ Comstock; E59(b), Jim Strawser/Grant Heilman Photography; E60, Tommaso Guicciardini/Photo Researchers; E61(bg), Donna Bise/Photo Researchers; E62, David Halpern/Photo Researchers; E63, Alan Pitcairn/Grant Heilman Photography; E64, Culver Pictures, Inc.; E65, U.S. Department of the Interior/ National Park Service, Saugus Iron Works National Historic Site; E66(t), Culver Pictures, Inc.; E66(b), U.S. Department of Energy; E67, U.S. Department of Energy; E68, Grant Heilman Photography; E69, UPI/Bettmann; E71, Runk/Schoenberger/Grant Heilman Photography; E71(bg), Leonard Lee Rue III/Earth Scenes; E72-E73(bg), Farrell Grehan/Photo Researchers; E73, Randall Hyman; E74(border), H. Armstrong Roberts, Inc.; E74(c), Ray Pfortner/Peter Arnold, Inc.; E74(inset), Grant Heilman/Grant Heilman Photography; E76(tl), Ray Pfortner/Peter Arnold, Inc.; E76(tr), Richard Weiss/Peter Arnold, Inc.; E76(bl), Clyde H. Smith/Peter Arnold, Inc.; E76(br), Walker/Peter Arnold, Inc.; E77(tl), Robert Winslow/Tom Stack & Assoc.; E77(tr), David Frazier/Sipa Press/ Air Products and Chemicals, Inc.; E77(bl), Matt Meadows/Peter Arnold, Inc.; E77(br), Doug Sokell/Tom Stack & Assoc.; E78(l), E78(b), Yann Arthus-Bertrand/Peter Arnold, Inc.; E79(l), Matthew Neal McVay/Tony Stone Images; E79(r), Barry L. Runk/ Grant Heilman Photography; E80(l), Francois Gohier/Photo Researchers; E80(r), Gerald A. Corsi/Tom Stack & Assoc.; E81(t), U.S. Department of Energy; E81(b), Hank Morgan/ Photo Researchers; E83, Bruno Barbey/Magnum Photos; E84, Steve McCurry/Magnum Photos; E85(r), Randy Brandon/Peter Arnold, Inc.; E85(b), Ann Duncan/Tom Stack & Assoc.; E87(t), Margaret McCarthy/Peter Arnold, Inc.; E87(b), Thomas Kitchin/Tom Stack & Assoc.; E88(border), National Snow and Ice Data Center/Photo Researchers; E88(c), E.R. Degginger/Color-Pic, Inc.; E88(inset), Mark Burnett/PhotoEdit; E89, William Felger/ Grant Heilman Photography; E92(t), E92(b), The Bettmann Archive; E93(t), Tom Pix/Peter Arnold, Inc.; E93(c), E93(b), Gerald A. Corsi/Tom Stack & Assoc.; E97, Erika Stone/Peter Arnold, Inc.; E98(l), Lawrence Migdale/Tony Stone Images; E98-E99, David M. Doody/Tom Stack & Assoc.; E100, David R. Frazier Photolibrary; E100-E101(bg), Pete Saloutos/Tony Stone Images; E101, Bill DeKay/ National Geographic Society; E102, Larry Voigt/Photo Researchers; E105(l), Dan Porges/Peter Arnold, Inc.; E105(r), Malcolm S. Kirk/Peter Arnold, Inc.; E106-E107(bg), Werner H. Muller/Peter Arnold, Inc.; E107(l), John Cancalosi/Tom Stack & Assoc.; E107(r), John Shaw/Tom Stack & Assoc.; E108-

E109(bg), Gerald A. Corsi/Tom Stack & Assoc.; E110(bl), David M. Dennis/Tom Stack & Assoc.; E110(br), Keith Kent/Peter Arnold, Inc.; E111(tl), Kevin Schafer/Tom Stack & Assoc.; E111(tr), Gary Milburn/Tom Stack & Assoc.; E111(bl), Brian Parker/Tom Stack & Assoc.; E111(br), Matt Meadows/Peter Arnold, Inc.; E112(l), IFA/Peter Arnold, Inc.; E112(r), Kevin Schafer/Peter Arnold, Inc.

Unit F. Harcourt Brace & Company Photographs: F4-F5, F7(t); F7(c); F7(b), Greg Leary; F8, F9, Photo Studio; F10-F11, F14, F15, F16, F19, F21(tl), Greg Leary; F21(tr), Photo Studio; F26(t), Greg Leary; F27, Maria Paraskavas; F30, F31, F32(t); F32(b), F37, F39, F42(l-inset), F43(bl); F45, F51, F53, F54, F56, F57, F58, F67, F68, F75, F77(l), F83, Greg Leary; F90, Weronica Ankarorn; F91(r); F92(t), Greg Leary; F92(b), Weronica Ankarorn; F93(t), F93(b), Greg Leary.

Unit F. All Other Photographs: Unit Divider Page, Comstock; F02-03(bg), Shirley Richards/Photo Researchers; F03, Joan Iaconetti/Bruce Coleman, Inc.; F06(t), Eunice Harris/Photo Researchers; F06(c), Alexander Lowry/Photo Researchers; F06(b), Rick Buettner/Bruce Coleman, Inc.; F12(border), Robert Frerck/Tony Stone Images; F12(c), F12(inset), SuperStock; F13(bg), H. Armstrong Roberts, Inc.; F14-15(bg), F18(tl), SIU/Photo Researchers; F18(tr), Norman Owen Tomalin/Bruce Coleman, Inc.; F18(br), Dr. Jeremy Burgess/Photo Researchers; F19(bg), Pasieka/Zefa/H. Armstrong Roberts, Inc.; F20, Ray Simons/Photo Researchers; F23, SuperStock; F26(bl), Jane Burton/Bruce Coleman, Inc.; F26(br), Richard Parker/Photo Researchers; F28, Judy McDuffy/Photo Researchers; F29, F33(t), Holt Confer/Grant Heilman Photography; F33(b), Joy Spurr/Bruce Coleman, Inc.; F35(t), SuperStock; F35(c), G. Büttner/Naturbild/OKAPIA/Photo Researchers; F35(b), Van Bucher/Photo Researchers; F36(border), Richard J. Green/Photo Researchers; F36(c), SuperStock; F36(inset), Michael P. Gadomski/Photo Researchers; F37(t), Steve Solum/ Bruce Coleman, Inc.; F38(t), Gilbert S. Grant/Photo Researchers; F38(b), Wardene Weisser/Bruce Coleman, Inc.; F40, SuperStock; F41(t), E.R. Degginger/Bruce Coleman, Inc.; F41(b), Dan Suzio/Photo Researchers; F42(tr), Bud Lehnhausen/Photo Researchers; F42(b), Lawrence Migdale/Photo Researchers; F43(tl), Lee Foster/Bruce Coleman, Inc.; F43(tr), SuperStock; F43(cr), G. Büttner/Naturbild/OKAPIA/Photo Researchers; F43(br), Erwin and Peggy Bauer/Bruce Coleman, Inc.; F44(border), Comstock; F44(c), E.R. Degginger/Photo Researchers; F44(inset), Bob & Clara Calhoun/Bruce Coleman, Inc.; F46, Rod Planck/Photo Researchers; F50(t), Anthony Mercieca/Photo Researchers; F50(c), J.H. Robinson/Photo Researchers; F50(cr), Hans Reinhard/Bruce Coleman, Inc.; F50(bl), SuperStock; F51(bg), D. Long/Visuals Unlimited; F52(bg), Alan L. Detrick/Photo Researchers; F55(t), F55(c), F55(b), Stephen J. Krasemann/Photo Researchers; F59(l), Wardene Weisser/Bruce Coleman, Inc.; F59(r), P. Munchenberg/SuperStock; F60(tr), Jane Burton/Bruce Coleman, Inc.; F60(l), Tom McHugh/Photo Researchers; F60-61, SuperStock; F61(tr), Uniphoto; F61(cl), John Kaprielian/Photo Researchers; F61(cr), Kenneth W. Fink/Photo Researchers; F63, Bettmann; F65, Pat Lanza/Bruce Coleman, Inc.; F66(border), Patricio Robles Gil/Bruce Coleman, Inc.; F66(c), SuperStock; F66(inset), Rod Planck/Photo Researchers; F69(b), Garry D. McMichael/Photo Researchers; F70(l), Waina Cheng/Bruce Coleman, Inc.; F70(r), John Shaw/Bruce Coleman, Inc.; F71(bg), Stephen P. Parker/Photo Researchers; F71(tl); F71(tc), John Kaprielian/ Photo Researchers; F71(tr), C.C. Lockwood/Bruce Coleman, Inc.; F71(cl), Stephen J. Krasemann/Photo Researchers; F71(cr), C.C. Lockwood/Bruce Coleman, Inc.; F71(bl), John Kaprielian/Photo Researchers; F72(l), D. Long/ Visuals Unlimited; F72(r), Jane Grushow/Grant Heilman Photography; F73(tl), Joy Spurr/Bruce Coleman, Inc.; F73(tr), Runk/Schoenberger/Grant Heilman Photography; F73(bl), D. Lada/H. Armstrong Roberts, Inc.; F73(br), Guy Gillette/ Photo Researchers; F74, SuperStock; F76(tr), John Kaprielian/Photo Researchers; F76(c), Nuridsanv et Pérennou/Photo Researchers; F76(cr), Alan L. Detrick/Photo Researchers; F76(br), Scott Camazine/Photo Researchers; F77(r), S. Nielsen/Bruce Coleman, Inc.; F78(t), Matt Bradley/Bruce Coleman, Inc.; F78(b), SuperStock; F79, Jen & Des Bartlett/Bruce Coleman, Inc.; F80(l), Wardene Weisser/Bruce Coleman, Inc.; F80(c), Jen & Des Bartlett/Bruce Coleman, Inc.; F80(r), John H. Hoffman/Bruce Coleman, Inc.; F81(t), Keith Gunnar/Bruce Coleman, Inc.; F81(l), Renee Lynn/Photo Researchers; F81(r), Rod Planck/Photo Researchers; F81(b), Gary R. Zahm/Bruce Coleman, Inc.; F82(r), SuperStock; F82(l), John Shaw/Bruce Coleman, Inc.; F82(br), Michael P. Gadomski/Bruce Coleman, Inc.; F84(tl), SuperStock; F84(tr), Douglas Faulkner/Photo Researchers; F84(bl), Mark N. Boulton/Photo Researchers; F84(bc), Len Rue Jr./Bruce Coleman, Inc.; F85(tl), J.H. Robinson/Photo Researchers; F85(tr), Dr. Paul A. Zahl/Photo Researchers; F85(bl), Stephen P. Parker/Photo Researchers; F85(br), Norm Thomas/Photo Researchers; F86(tl), SuperStock; F86(tr), Robert P. Carr/Bruce Coleman, Inc.; F86(cl), Renee Lynn/Photo Researchers; F86(bl), John M. Burnley/Photo Researchers; F86(bc), Joy Spurr/Bruce Coleman, Inc.; F86(inset), Terry Ross/Visuals Unlimited; F86-87, Hans Reinhard/Bruce Coleman, Inc.; F87(r), Kim Taylor/Bruce Coleman, Inc.; F87(c), SuperStock; F88, Minnesota Landscape Arboretum; F89, Dennis Carlyle Darling-Holt, Rinehart & Winston; F90-91(bg), S. Nielsen/Bruce Coleman, Inc.; F91(tl), Tim Davis/Photo Researchers; F91(tc), Robert E. Pelham/Bruce Coleman, Inc.; F92-93(bg), H. Abernathy/H. Armstrong Roberts, Inc.; F94(t), Michael P. Gadomski/Bruce Coleman, Inc.; F94(b), SuperStock; F95(l), John E. Sass/Photo Researchers; F95(cl), Gilbert S. Grant/Photo Researchers; F95(cr), Michael S. Renner/Bruce Coleman, Inc.; F95(r), Runk/Schoenberger/Grant Heilman Photography

Reference Handbook. Harcourt Brace & Company Photographs: R4(all), Ralph J. Brunke; R5(b), Weronica Ankarorn; R9, Earl Kogler; R7(all); R8, R10(all), R11, R12, R13, R14, R15, R16, R17, R19, Ralph J. Brunke.

Reference Handbook. All Other Photographs: R5(t), Science Kit & Boreal Laboratories.